I AM MY CULTURE:

My Memoir of Self-Determination

Published in Canada by
Celestial Publishing and Media

ISBN 978-1-7389143-0-2

Back cover art: Jimmy Boulanger
Author photo: Brandy Bloxom Photography
Cover and interior design: Iris Cameron
Editing: Sheila Cameron

Type set in Adobe Caslon Pro, Avenir, and Costa STD

I AM MY CULTURE:

My Memoir of Self-Determination

A JOURNAL FOR WELL-BEING

Annette Alix Roussin, MSW

Acknowledgements

I am grateful and say miigwech to my parents and siblings, my husband, son and daughters, my friends, extended family, my community, the Miimiiwiziibiing (Berens River First Nation) Education Committee, and all my relations. I say miigwech to my Elder Margaret Lavallee for her constant support and teachings. Miigwech to my circle of support who assisted me on my path with the writing, editing, and design of this memoir journal. Miigwech to Victoria Johnson, PhD and Celestial Publishing and Media for being an ally and supporting my work and our relationship toward Truth and Reconciliation.

Content warning
The author includes research that discusses aspects of colonization and how it has affected her personally. If any part of her story or the research is upsetting to readers, they are encouraged to use the journal spaces to process their thoughts, feelings, and experiences, or to find someone safe with whom they can process their feelings.

Note
The author uses the word Indigenous to encapsulate First Nations, Métis peoples, Non-Status, and Inuit. Readers can self-identify as Indigenous or choose how they identify themselves.

Table of Contents

Preface

My writing is a caption of how I experienced my evolvement with my cultural identity, which I misunderstood for much of my life. Once I learned about colonization and the aspects of forced assimilation and systemic racism, I was able to connect this knowledge with my low self-esteem and bouts of depression. Despite this knowledge, it became a personal responsibility to find healing. I had to find a way to keep moving forward without negating what I knew about the history and its harsh realities. I had to do the work to learn about self-love and balance. I had to learn how to think better of myself and reframe the label of low self-esteem. I had to overcome internalized oppression.

I completed the first five years of my sobriety while attending university. I used many different self-help books for self-awareness and understanding to support my self-determination. I enjoyed the process of participating in twelve-step groups, and I felt like I belonged. I received therapy from professionals who helped me process the changes I needed and wanted to make in my life. My healing path led me to learning more about my cultural history and embracing all the strengths that come from my Indigenous culture.

As the years passed, I wanted to stop the intergenerational transmission of historical colonial effects. I decided I would become a therapist because I found a real passion in helping others heal. The path to commit to my education in the Faculty of Social Work unfolded as I continued forward. My social work education gave me the credentials to support my becoming a therapist. This was a great fit for me because I wanted to do my part to help decrease racism and oppression and increase self-determination, self-awareness, self-acceptance, and self-love.

My story is about growth and change. It includes my experiences with cultural reclamation, self-determination, self-love, and personal growth work. It is the sharing of memories, stories, and strategies I have incorporated into my life that have become my spiritual bundle.

Writing my memoir and creating it into this journal has been a part of my ongoing healing journey. Letting go of the fear of vulnerability to write and share my opinions and perspectives was difficult. Pursuing this creative project has supported my growth and strengthened my mental well-being and sense of balance.

I have journaled regularly since approximately 1996. Experiencing a history of colonization and confusion about my cultural identity along with my low moods really drained my energy. It hurt me physically, mentally, emotionally, and spiritually. There were many days I carried this pain around inside of me and I did not have someone available to talk to about what I was feeling, or I did not feel comfortable enough to say out loud to someone what I was thinking and feeling. My journal became a trusted friend where I could share all my thoughts and feelings that kept going around and around in my head.

I recognized journaling as a helpful healing strategy I could use while acknowledging the systemic oppressive structures of colonialism. I journaled how I had internalized the colonial experience and how it caused me to think less of myself and how I oppressed myself and others without even knowing this is what I was doing. There was a time in my life that I did not even know this about myself. I did not know there were instances where I had become the oppressor!

I searched for journals to write in where I could share what was occurring for me as an Indigenous, Ojibway, mixed-blood, cisgender, heterosexual woman, but I could not find a journal that included such topics for consideration. I also could not find a book on Indigenous topics that included space to write in when my issues or past trauma experiences were activated or when I knew they were related to my experiences and my cultural identity.

My journaling helped me establish balance and harmony in my life. I began to understand myself at a deeper level, and I changed. I continued to move beyond challenges that had stemmed from the historical effects of colonization here in Canada. After I completed my Master of Social Work, and after years of practicing in various positions using my professional training as a social worker to help others, I decided to complete my memoir. Parts of my life and situations that I recalled were related to how I felt about myself and my Indigenous identity. I began to see the possibility that my stories—combined with

> I wrote this book as a gift to myself and my inner child, the young girl within me who at the age of ten or eleven years old wanted to write, and to honour my healing journey and those who have helped me along the way.

2

journaling prompts—might be helpful to others on their healing journeys. By listening to my spirit and desire, I understood it was time to create the space I had so wanted and needed for myself.

This memoir journal has become a part of my story to wholeness and an opportunity to pay it forward. I want to share hope with anyone who connects with my story to help them know that they are not alone. We are interconnected. Through the interconnectedness we have with one another, and through self-awareness and reflection, this personal action can be life changing.

Introduction

During my graduate studies program in social work, and the years I practiced as a clinical social worker in the post-secondary, public school system and in Aboriginal health, I continuously focused my research on Indigenous (First Nations, Métis peoples, Non-Status, and Inuit) mental health and how the process of colonization has affected Indigenous Peoples' mental health and well-being. This was my focus because by the age of twelve I knew I had my own struggles with how I was feeling about myself, and my mood was often low. My personal interest and my spirit naturally gravitated me toward becoming a champion for Indigenous mental health and well-being. Therefore, I chose different positions on my career path that gave me the opportunity to learn, research, and understand what was affecting our Indigenous mental health and well-being. I had sat and listened to many Indigenous people to know this was important work that needed to be done. It became my purpose for my vocation and guided my own self-determination. The literature I gathered began to paint a picture of the historical effects of colonization on Indigenous Peoples and its negative effects on those colonized livelihoods.

My use of the term colonization defines the historical processes of what happened on Turtle Island in Canada when settlers arrived many centuries ago and began to govern and rule the land and people, namely the Indigenous Peoples they say were "found." The colonialist governmental rule orchestrated the marginalization and oppression of Indigenous Peoples in collaboration with the various churches through organized religions to take over the country and its resources and its Peoples. In doing this, the settlers secured themselves in a position of power and privilege. This was the origin of systemic oppression.

My research supports the critique that colonialism remains as a contributor to the continuous strife for Indigenous Peoples' livelihood and mental well-being. Colonialism, based in racism and discriminatory policies, continues to perpetuate the subjugation of Indigenous Peoples. The history of the Indian residential schools and the colonial assimilation policies have had devastating effects, and the pursuit of

4

Indigenous Peoples to overcome colonialism and its effects is ongoing. As I write, many Indigenous children's unmarked graves at the sites of former Indian residential schools have been uncovered, and many Indigenous Peoples are reliving the pain and have been retraumatized.

There is no denying that colonization set the foundation for systemic racism and oppression to thrive, grow, and solidify. The negative aftereffect of early colonization continues to echo throughout many generations. This is what is called the intergenerational effects of the Indian residential school system.

The self-determination and esteem of the children, parents and communities who lived and survived during these eras have had much to overcome. As these children—the Survivors of the Indian residential schools who grew up and became adults with this shared history of their negative experiences—tried to move forward with their own lives into mainstream society or back to their communities, they were left navigating deep wounds. How could these atrocities—such as having their children removed and taken to the Indian residential schools, being dispossessed from the land and their communities, or being punished for using the traditional practices of ceremony and speaking their language—not negatively influence mental well-being, sense of self, attachments to one another, familial relationships, and community cohesiveness? I've had my own experience with cultural confusion, low self-esteem, and feelings of not belonging and self-hate that developed into mistrust and feelings of unworthiness. I've learned that the issues I had through being born into my family and my life are related to colonization.

I am not going to delve into governmental bureaucracy and policies or the many complexities of colonization, such as the history of the treaties when Canada was settled, or any current political situations. Colonization is a humongous and complex topic, and there are many other people—like my sister, Joan Jack—who continuously participate in cultural advocacy and dedicate their lives to the unravelling and revealing of the historical and current reality of the relationships with Indigenous Peoples.

Nor will I revisit every memory or personal trauma I have experienced based on my identifying as an Indigenous, Ojibway, mixed-blood, cisgender, heterosexual woman. My family of origin consisted of my mom, dad and two siblings, an older sister, and a younger brother and myself. Dad has passed on and Mom is doing well in her senior years. She is strong, vibrant, creative, and free. I had grandparents and have cousins on both sides of my family, and they all have their own stories. I've done my best to be respectful and tell only my story as an individual, mother, wife, sister, family and community member, friend, middle-class, able-bodied, recovered alcoholic, and multiple trauma Survivor.

In this memoir journal, I share my experience in learning about being colonized and how being born into it has affected me personally. I have written it not in a linear way, which is often the way of colonialism, but in a way that suits me and follows my own internal path of what was relevant and important for me to share in its creation. I have made the choice to simply tell aspects of my story so that others may have the opportunity to think about their family of origin or to journal about their own story associated with colonization.

Although my parents did not attend the Indian residential schools, they did attend what was called the day school system. The day school system was governed and operated by the Roman Catholic Church. My parents' experiences had an intergenerational effect on me, and this is what I will continue to share about as I include my personal perceptions connected to the historical reality.

I know this history affected me and my psyche. Therefore, I make this effort to share my story and how it is possible to survive and thrive through this historical attempt to eradicate our cultural ways and separate us from our Traditional Knowledge. As a child, I learned lessons both spoken and unspoken that to be seen as Indigenous was not the way one wanted to be. The process of decolonizing my mind and life periodically feels like a real challenge as the colonial neural pathways are so deeply embedded in my brain. It is a consistent feeling of stepping in and out of the Western and Indigenous worlds, on two paths, and sometimes it probably even has the physiological effect relative to my issues with hypertension and anxiety.

In a study about racial discrimination, post-traumatic stress disorder (PTSD), and prescription drug problems among Indigenous Canadians, Currie et al. (2015) explain it is important to consider what experiencing discrimination on an ongoing basis does to one's overall emotional or mental health, but also to one's overall physical or physiological health. Lewis, Cogburn and Williams (2015) in Currie et al. argue there is evidence that people experiencing discriminatory practices or racism on an ongoing basis have higher rates of heart disease, age faster, and have induced endocrine function. Currie et al. acknowledge studies which indicate that continuous experiences of discrimination and racism do increase the use of substances as a coping mechanism for some, and over time this becomes an issue of generational substance abuse.[1]

Few studies have been conducted on how discrimination is associated with symptoms of PTSD. Still, the conclusion drawn from the Currie et al. (2015) research is that many Indigenous people do experience higher levels of racial discrimination, and that discrimination is linked to symptoms of PTSD. Thus, many Indigenous people begin using prescription drugs to mask their physical and emotional pain and simply to cope with life because of racism and discrimination. Many Indigenous Peoples are living in the margins of society and the resulting socio-economic status has affected their overall health as they experience issues of poverty, classism, racism, and continued oppression through colonialism.

The intergenerational effects of collective trauma have been passed to several families and communities within and across generations. Though many of the historical experiences of Indigenous Peoples have not been studied or validated by empirical research, I argue that colonization still is the experiential reality of Indigenous Peoples today. Indigenous individuals and families are experiencing increased levels of stress, suicide rates, and incidents of various types of physical, sexual, and emotional abuse, as well as lower levels of socio-economic status and higher incidents of racism as compared to non-Indigenous people who have not undergone generations of historical trauma, collective oppression, and marginalization within their own country of origin.

Many Indigenous people have experienced loss of culture, its knowledge, values, language, pride, and the fundamental connection to the land-base. This was the goal of the colonial government in Canada. If these attributes were not completely lost or hidden to be safe from retribution and possible incarceration, they (were ignored or) may have been wrapped in layers of cultural self-shame, fear, and confusion and therefore ignored.

Consequently, these historical legal and political realities led to many Indigenous Peoples—me included—internalizing the external systemized oppression. The result was a manifestation of mental health issues and poor overall health outcomes. In other words, many Indigenous Peoples have internalized the systemic racism and oppression and now blame themselves and each other for much of the historic and collective traumatic experiences. This internalized oppression is a driver of feelings of low self-esteem, worthlessness, suicidal ideation,

7

alcoholism, and addiction that many Indigenous people suffer with today. I felt this way; I felt my spirit was broken or wounded, and I began to understand I had many challenges to overcome.

Colonialism and oppression can break a person's spirit and it is a constant challenge to overcome these external stressors that play havoc on an internal psyche and well-being. This understanding I now have is what gives me strength and hope to create a safe space where a person can share their story. I hope the reader will use my memoir journal as a tool and support in a space that acknowledges the effects of colonization and oppression.

My memoir journal can be used by anyone who suffers or has suffered with negative thoughts about themselves. It is for anyone who may think or feel that negative circumstances and experiences in their story could be connected to colonization in Canada. It is for any person who has internalized their oppression. I want the journal to give them space to explore what this means to them personally.

It is my hope for you as the reader to engage with the space provided to self-reflect and process your own story. My hope is that you will use the journal spaces and that you can use my story for increasing your own awareness, well-being, and to honour your story and journey. If you self-identify as Indigenous, I hope it will help you to see yourself as a beautiful, strong spirit with many gifts and strengths.

Maybe you do not have the same issues I have had. Maybe you feel whole, balanced, and complete, and reading this memoir journal will give you space to acknowledge all your accomplishments and gifts to honour yourself and your family to create more dreams you want to build upon. As you read on, you can use the journal spaces to reflect on what this might mean to you in your story and life experiences. You will have the opportunity to capture what is occurring for you in your own life story. The space will be there to journal and articulate your emotions and memories. If there is emotional pain you need to release, I hope you can free yourself from wounds and process safely what you might be carrying. If you find you need support, I encourage you to seek a friend or person to read this memoir journal with together.

Likewise, you may also remember the good in your life and take time to write about this too. Our good thoughts and memories keep us strong and well. You may also want to journal about what your strengths are, where they come from, or perhaps what you have overcome or are in the process of overcoming. You might want to pursue or create your own Medicine Wheel plan for your life. Whatever way you choose to immerse yourself in the memoir journal stories will be perfect for you at this time, and you can always revisit any part when you think or feel it is necessary.

I Am My Culture is also written for those who are non-Indigenous. You may be non-Indigenous and have thoughts and feelings about the history of colonization and your relationship with Indigenous Peoples in Canada. You may see yourself as an ally for justice, change, and diversity respective to Indigenous Peoples in Canada. Or you could be just beginning to realize you carry many stereotypes and prejudices toward Indigenous Peoples. I invite you to read my memoir journal and use the space for self-reflection. Until people who are non-Indigenous start looking at themselves through self-awareness and reflection, nothing changes.

There are many different realities for us all. I have often heard my sister, Joan Jack, say, "We are all trees; some are poplar, some are birch or pine." My reality is both complex and simple at the same time, and I am forever evolving. My culture, my identity, and my healing journey are what bring me to this place of honouring my past and loving myself today. My hope is for us to see one another; I want to see you and you to see me. It is through our interconnectedness that healing happens. It is through acknowledging our differences and accepting difference that I think there is an opportunity for positive change. I know I do not have to be like anyone else now and I need to be "me" and that my culture is something to be honoured and valued.

I share with you who I am to create the space to process through journaling what is important and relevant for you. We all have a purpose and gifts to share with each other and I know I am worthy; we are all worthy. I acknowledge the fact that reciprocal relationships are one of the most important aspects of my culture. I am an interdependent human being. I have learned I have relationships with the land, the animals, objects both animate and inanimate, and the sky, the moon, and the sun just to name a few.

Journal Space: Can you relate to what I have shared so far, about how colonization and external experiences and systems have affected my inner self? Take some time to honour yourself and your story and write about what colonization and its effects mean to you.

East – The Beginning

I have chosen to name the direction of East as the beginning of my story. The sun rises in the east every morning and I wake up to knowing it is there whether I see it or not. I have learned to wake up each morning and begin my day knowing I am living in my Medicine Wheel of life—the physical, mental, emotional, and spiritual parts of me and in my life.

Despite the Canadian colonialist reality, there is strength and hope through the sharing of our stories, our connectedness, and our personal choices. We are all unique human beings, but I believe that accepting our differences and respecting this reality is where connections can occur, and we can share and gain strength.

The combination of knowledge I gathered from my academic journey, the use of self-help materials, and the willingness to embrace cultural knowledge has helped me understand myself and supported my cultural reclamation. This process deepened my love and compassion for self and others. I used it to heal my internalized racism and sustain my physical, mental, emotional, and spiritual well-being. The path was there in front of me, and I am so grateful I kept choosing to do my inner work throughout the years. Going inward to learn about who I was and why I was behaving in various ways is possibly the greatest endeavour I've undertaken. I recommend this healing journey to anyone.

I learned how to feel my feelings, let them flow through me, and take care of myself in healthier ways. My thoughts and feelings can range from being like a calm, flowing river to a raging river or to varying degrees between. I have learned to accept this reality and love myself while I am in the process of trying to understand what is occurring for me. I have learned to ask myself the question, "What do I need to do in this moment or situation?" Now when my emotions are volatile—like there is a storm brewing in me or I am unusually low—I no longer feel victimized or trapped. Instead, I feel empowered to find the answers I need within myself.

At different points in my journey, I felt discouraged because I received feedback to stop thinking about my life and my work from such an individualistic perspective since I come from a collective culture. At least this is how I heard the advice at the time it was given to me, and I did not ask for further clarification. I disagreed with these opinions and instead made the decision to accept myself, stay on my path, and keep moving forward. I learned afterward that the idea of individualism is from a colonialist worldview. But choosing to do something for myself which I genuinely believed was in my collective worldview was from my own volition and an act of self-determination. I felt called by my spirit to restore the sacredness of relationships and this included honouring myself and what I desired to accomplish. I used the healing strength I had already gained to honour and make my own decision and let go of the external feedback. I listened to my spirit guiding me forward. Colonization is a part of the reality I live in. The more I understand about my history and Indigenous cultural practices and release the negative effects of the colonial experience, the more I remember to stay calm and not listen to negative thoughts that would keep me in the experience of cultural shame and low self-esteem.

Now I believe and understand there is no wrong path; there is only a path which we each must walk. And this story is my path. This is my gift and the strength I bring forward and this is what my Creator wants for me. I am grateful to be alive and well and giving myself the permission to put my words and thoughts on paper. I hope that this might give others who identify with my story the strength and courage to keep on their path to do their inner work and grow in their own self-determination, self-love, peace, and healing. When one of us heals due to our interconnectedness I believe we all benefit.

Who Am I?

I was born and raised in a small remote community in central Manitoba and am a registered citizen of Miimiiwiziibiing (Berens River First Nation) Treaty No. 5. I am the middle child with one older sister and one younger brother. Our mother was raised with the surname McKay. I have limited memories of my childhood, and I am aware that my siblings have their own perceptions of their childhood and our family.

I latched onto loneliness and sadness in my early years. As far back in my childhood as I can remember, the one feeling I recall the most was sadness. I felt sad a lot. I felt there was something wrong with me, like I did not belong. I do not know how factual this is nor am I aware whether people noticed this about me, but I do remember feeling like this often. When I look through old photographs from my youth, it reminds me of the fun picnics, boat rides, or games I was involved with that did bring me joy. But, deep inside I had the ongoing struggle with how I was feeling, so I had learned at a very young age to mask my feelings.

However, I know my childhood was not entirely spent in sadness. There were many happy times. I remember as a little girl I would run over to my friend's house. If it was hot outside, the front door would be wide open, and I would go flying through it into the middle of the kitchen. There I would bump right into my friend's mom sweeping the kitchen floor. She'd have her apron on and her dish towel hanging over her shoulder, her long, shiny, black hair wrapped in a bun on the top of her head. The radio would be playing some old country song by George

Me at age two

Jones or Loretta Lynn. My friend's mom would greet me with love and a big warm smile and—as soon as I could catch my breath—I would ask her if she had any bannock. She would laugh and say, "You know where it is. Go help yourself."

You bet I knew where it was. I knew where the bannock drawer was, and I headed straight to it. I felt the drawer handle in my little hand, and I pulled open that drawer made of old weathered plywood with laminate tablecloth cut to line the bottom of it. I peered in and sometimes I would have to stick my arm far into the drawer and feel around. If I only felt crumbs, it meant I would have to stretch even further as it was a long, flat, deep drawer. I would finally feel the bannock, and I would smile to myself as my fingers connected with its texture. I could hardly wait to eat. I took the knife out of the drawer and cut myself a piece. My lips were parted, and my saliva was building as I cut that bannock. Then my eyes would move to the top of the cupboard hoping to find the butter and jam to go with it. I loved these times, and I would savour the texture, taste, and nourishing love I felt when I got to have some. I did not feel judged; all I felt was my friend's mom's generosity, love, and acceptance.

I also remember eating rabbit soup at our kookum's house. Kookum is the Saulteaux/Ojibwe word I was taught to use as my grandmother's name—my mother's mother—and I always loved visiting her and my grandfather. The Saulteaux/Ojibwe word for grandfather is mishoomis, but I did not learn to use this word until later in my adulthood. When I spoke to my grandfather as a child, I would use the English word and addressed him as grandpa. We could only go to our kookum's house by boat because we lived on an island. This was doubly exciting—not only did we get to visit our grandparents, but we also got a fun boat ride.

I remember visits to my grandparent's place were the best. I felt special there and my grandparents had given me a special name, which was "Baby Ann." My kookum had puffy, tough-skinned hands, always wore an apron, and often had her nylons rolled down to rest around her ankles. She gave the best hugs. I loved to be near her and sit and rub those hard-working hands and savour the smell of her rabbit soup on the stove. One of my favourite childhood treasures was the furry, lucky rabbit's foot I got to keep after my kookum had skinned and cleaned a rabbit to make her delicious soup. After everyone ate, I would sit with my cousins on the kitchen floor near my kookum and play the fun game of spin the rabbit's head with the boiled rabbit skull. We would make up some type of task you had to do or say if the rabbit skull jaw landed pointing at you.

Out back of my kookum's house were big flat rocks with a lot of moss and crusty plant growth. I loved to go out there with my cousins, feeling free and having so much fun playing hide and seek or just running around being a kid with no worries whatsoever. On the rare occasion I recall there were visits to my other aunt's homes—in our culture, we called them Grandma too. They also lived on the same side of the river as my kookum, so it was a real treat to get to run through the bush trails to go and visit them. I remember I felt so happy watching my Grandma May do her beading and it was such a special time to be able to visit her house, or seeing Grandma Billy and just to be near her was so special.

Grandpa was often outside, sitting and sorting his fishing nets. I would sit near him and watch how he would work to take out all the knots and sticks and other things that were caught in the nets as he prepared them for the next time they would go out and set them again. Grandpa loved to tease; this was his way of showing and telling us he loved us.

My parents operated one of the grocery stores in the community. In my view, they worked hard. Mom is Indigenous and identified as Métis when she was younger. Her identity changed over time, but that is her story to tell, not mine. My dad's parents were Lebanese and English, but my dad was raised in Manitoba in the community of Little Grand Rapids where they sang with the drum and danced and did the ceremonies when he was a little boy. My father was non-Indigenous but spoke fluent Saulteaux/Ojibwe and had these childhood experiences. My parents attended schools operated by the Catholic Church that are now called day schools, which meant they could come home to their families at night. However, the Catholic Church day schools had the same mandate as the Indian residential schools, and this was to convert and oppress all aspects of cultural and collective Indigenous ways the children may have had.

My parents were taught Catholicism and expected to speak English. Even though Dad was non-Indigenous, he was still subjected to the message it was bad or wrong to speak the Saulteaux/Ojibwe language. I believe this affected my parents' mental health, self-esteem and how they interacted with one another and later how they parented us. They may not have understood the role the effects of day school and colonialism played in their lives and in their marriage, and I don't think they ever realized how that may have connected with struggles in their relationship. Their relationship and interaction with one another seemed complex.

Please feel free to draw or doodle anything that comes up for you. This is your memoir journal.

Journal Space: Do you have any childhood memories connected to your family of origin and why you are the way you are? Take the time to honour yourself and your story and write what it means to you.

There was this unspoken reality of racism occurring within the Canadian social context and within our community when I was a child. Indian residential schools first opened in Canada in the first quarter of the nineteenth century around 1828. The network was funded by the Canadian government's Department of Indian Affairs and administered by the Christian Church. It was mandatory for Indigenous children to attend residential schools in Canada from 1894 to 1946. The last school was Kivalliq Hall in Rankin Inlet which closed in 1997.

The Catholic Church was influential in my family of origin. My grandparents had been indoctrinated into it. During my childhood and into the beginning of my youth, my family attended Mass regularly. I went to catechism, did first Communion, and was confirmed. It was a way of life, and my family participated regularly as practicing Catholics.

My grandparents spoke their Saulteaux language with other speakers but did not speak in the language to me and did not share with me who we were as a cultural people. I realized much later that they were living and modelling their values and the culture in more general ways through their generosity, hunting, fishing, humour, and kindness to others.

My parents were fluent in the Saulteaux language that they had both learned to speak in their childhoods, but I think they made the conscious decision not to teach it to me and my siblings to protect us from racism due to their own history of being oppressed and punished for speaking the language. I have memories of being corrected to "speak properly" and to "speak English" whenever I would use any type of slang. I internalized this and picked up an unspoken feeling of being ashamed of being Indigenous, and this is where my cultural shame started.

At the same time, derogatory and prejudiced comments about "being Indian"—or as we now call ourselves, Indigenous—increased the shame associated with being Indigenous. These experiences caused me to try and remain as quiet and unnoticeable as I possibly could and to disassociate from anything or anyone Indigenous as it seemed to me the goal was to follow the Catholic Church's rules and speak proper English as best I could. This is one of the intergenerational effects of colonization that occurred, although I did not recognize it at the time.

Contributing to my feelings of not belonging, I have vague memories of hearing conversations amongst adults in the community about "who was Indian and who was not." If I tried to speak our cultural language, I would sometimes be ridiculed by my Indigenous peers. In this way, I felt "not good enough to speak our language," and so I stopped trying. I felt confused about who I was, vacillating between feeling either not White enough or not Indigenous enough. I did not feel good about myself at all and hid this and many other feelings.

Our community was divided by land allocation between the provincial government where the Métis lived, and the federal government reserve land, and land owned by the Catholic Church. We lived on an island until I was eight years old and didn't know which land base I belonged to. This contributed to my sense of not belonging and affected how I interacted with others. Logistically, we could not be with other children or families easily because we were on this island, and it kept us apart. It took a lot of effort for my parents to let us have friends over to play because they would have to make a trip by boat to transport the children back and forth from our island to the mainland. However, when I did get to have a day with friends or cousins on the island with us, it was so much fun! Our island was so small that when we played on the swings that my dad had made for us, it seemed we would be able to fly off the swing into the river as we were going back and forth. I think my dad felt the same way as I can remember him cautioning us to not swing too hard or high when we were playing.

Later, my parents moved the store to the mainland where we lived on land they managed to purchase from the Catholic Church. My parents had to spend many hours in the store to make it a success. All three of us children also worked in the store when we were not in school. I remember one of the jobs I had with my sister while we waited for the school bus was to sweep the cement pad at the store's front doors so it would be clean for customers every morning when the store opened. One time, we got our hands on some chalk and decided to play hopscotch while waiting for the school bus. Playing like this in the early mornings with my sister was so much fun, but our escapade did not go over well with Dad because it made the storefront pad look messy to him, so we quickly had to stop with the chalk!

I constantly wanted to leave the store to play with friends and to go for visits with my cousins, but there was not a lot of time for such things. This also contributed to my feeling lonely and disconnected or of not belonging. Family gatherings, picnics, and spending time together in leisurely interaction was not the norm for us. I internalized the expectation that to stay close to home and work in the store was our norm.

Contributing to my confusion was my reality of not having the challenge of lacking any basic needs. Our parents had installed our own water and electricity when we lived on the island. I carried guilt and shame for having the basic amenities like running water because I was fully aware that many of my relatives and friends did not. I was the daughter of the storekeeper which situated me within the community differently compared to others. Colonialism and economics affected how I thought of myself and how I thought others perceived me.

Two other occurrences that affected my sense of well-being were my parents' divorce after almost twenty-five years of marriage, and my older sister having to leave home so she could attend high school. To this day, there is still no high school in Berens River. My mother and sister moved out of our family home, and I was left with my father and my little brother who was nine years younger than me. I felt immense loss and abandonment when this happened. However, I had mixed emotions over my sister leaving. On one hand, I was excited to have our bedroom all to myself but on the other hand, I really missed her and felt as though she, too, had abandoned me.

Being so young—I was twelve when this happened—these changes were difficult to comprehend. I do not have completely clear memories of every aspect of my childhood. I think this is partly due to some of the negative emotions I felt, and situations I saw or experienced. Partly it is from the passage of time—I just don't remember; the memories have faded away. But the family dynamics with Mom and my sister moving away created a real challenge for me to feel connected to the two of them for many years. I quickly fell into a role of being my brother's and father's keeper. I have vague recollections of a sense of over-responsibility for my father and brother, whether it was perceived or real.

I know I did the best I could to be the good daughter and sister and not cause any extra grief or stress for our father at this time. I blamed my mom's moving away for some of what I was feeling. She would try to connect with me, but my sense of abandonment and blame toward her were extraordinarily strong, so I pushed her away for the most part. Our mother had left the community and began to become involved in Métis politics. Her Indigenous roots were another reason I did not want to be with her. This is how my internalized "cultural self-hatred" had manifested, and I am sure I also picked up some negative judgements from my father about our mom leaving. In my opinion, I believe he passed away without ever forgiving Mom for leaving the marriage, and I do not believe he ever admitted to having played a role in the ending of their marriage. However, these are my personal reflections, and I do not know the truth behind my parents' relationship and its breakdown.

Another feeling I quickly internalized as a child was guilt. I constantly felt guilty for wanting to participate in normal childhood activities like playing. It somehow felt bad, and having fun was also wrong. Internalized cultural confusion creates these issues. The only type of activity that received any positive affirmation in our home was work. I started to work in our store regularly at the age of twelve. Often when I missed Dad or other family members, I would go and join my dad working in the store. This was the only way I got to spend time with him and feel connected. I also became a mini coordinator. I realized that since I had to work and I could not go out to play with my friends, I would ask my best friend to come and be with me in the store to keep me company. I would also help sort the store inventory kept in the basement of our house, and my friend would help me do this work and then we would sneak in a bit of play. These opportunities were acceptable and made me happy. They seemed to alleviate my feelings of being left out when I learned my friends were going for a boat ride with their family or when there was a baseball game I couldn't attend.

I am aware I had issues associated with my cultural identity and I was literally suffering from cultural self-hate, and I lacked a sense of belonging. These "issues" I had later manifested into coping behaviours such as substance abuse, people pleasing, and workaholism.

I often felt guilty and ashamed when I wanted to relax and read books. I used to hide in my bedroom to read. I loved the Nancy Drew series that had been left in our house by my sister. I felt guilty for lying down to read and enjoy myself. I often wonder if this guilt had its origins from the Catholic religion which influenced how our parents raised us. The message was to be seen and not heard. I do know my father did not have much use for education because of his experience in the day school as a child. He shared with me how before he attended school, he had fun playing with his friends, hunting birds or other little animals and they would skin and cook them up on small campfires. This is where he learned much of the Saulteaux language. But, once he started school, he and his peers were punished for speaking Saulteaux and felt the fear and judgement of the nuns who taught them. We had discussions about his Grade 4 education, and as soon as he was able to quit school and go to work in the store his father operated, he did. From that point, he was a self-taught businessman because once he was able to work, he did not have to go to school anymore. Over time, if there was anything he needed to learn, he would read Popular Mechanic magazines and talk to other men or people who might know more about what he needed to learn. He watched how his parents operated the store and began to take leadership in this area in his family.

My thoughts here reflect several generations of my family who are affected by colonization and the interaction between the church and the state. I believe both my grandparents and my parents were not allowed to play and have fun as children. They were taught that to speak their language, play, have fun, and to have creative experiences was wrong, lazy, and shameful. The message they often internalized was "you are lazy and unworthy if you do not work." This message was taught to them as children, and it was passed on from one generation to another. Being playful and imaginative for the sake of pure joy was wrong. As I grew up, I had this big gaping hole inside of me, layered with guilt, shame, and a sense of woundedness for being the me who wanted to play and to be creative.

Please feel free to draw or doodle anything that comes up for you. This is your memoir journal.

Journal Space: Do you have any guilt, shame, or woundedness? Take some time to honour yourself and your story and write what it means to you.

_____
_____
_____
_____
_____
_____
_____
_____
_____
_____
_____
_____
_____
_____
_____
_____
_____
_____
_____
_____
_____
_____
_____
_____
_____
_____
_____
_____
_____
_____
_____
_____
_____
_____
_____
_____

Seeking Belonging

I was continuously looking for something to fill this hole I had inside me and to fix my wounded spirit. When I was about fourteen and searching for that place and space, I tried out various religious groups. I learned about a different type of Christianity other than Catholicism through a friend of our father. This man and his family were part of an evangelical church. On the suggestion of my dad's friend, I attended some of their services and tried to connect with some of the youth I met there. I even underwent a form of baptism in their church. When I went home to my community afterward, I went to my kookum's to have my usual visit. I was very excited to see her and share what I had experienced meeting the new youth and undergoing this water baptism. To my shock, my kookum was angered. I remember her saying, "You are Catholic, and this is wrong. If you choose to follow this type of religion, then you are no longer my grandchild!"

Although the religious spaces I tried did not feel comfortable for me, I also felt rejected by my kookum for trying them. I did not feel comfortable in her presence afterward, and I felt doubly confused because I could see my grandparents were Indigenous and this meant I was Indigenous. In hindsight, I now see I had internalized cultural self-hate without even understanding it was occurring. I was also being rejected for something that my dad's friend had suggested might help me with my feelings of loss and confusion.

For the most part, I was quiet and shy. I tried my best to just fit in and go unnoticed as much as possible. I did my best to be the "good girl" so people would love and accept me. I now realize this is how I became an approval seeker and a people pleaser. I so badly wanted to fit in and be loved, but I had already internalized the message that I was unlovable and unworthy. My parents periodically told me they loved me, but it just did not sink in. I do not recall any messages such as, "You are so beautiful," or "I love you just the way you are" from either parent in our home. I also do not recall them saying loving messages to one another in my presence. I do not know what my parents thought and felt about being parents or how they decided to parent. My guess is they—like many other people— did the best they could, based on what they had experienced as children in their own families of origin. I learned at such a young age to be dutiful and obedient, to be a people pleaser to be liked, loved, and accepted. I remember there were moments when I wished I were ill because then maybe someone would love me and pay attention to me.

My feelings of inadequacy and shame became amplified in adolescence. While adolescence is naturally a time of awkwardness, I felt I was the only one who felt this way. To add to my challenges, my father constantly conveyed the message that being skinny was better and more acceptable. I have memories of what I think was him nagging our mother about his ideas of how good it was to be thin. I think this affected her mental well-being because it seemed Mom was constantly dieting or trying to change herself. Over time, I internalized this message and believed I had to be thin to earn his approval, love, and acceptance.

The combination of feeling judged and unacceptable as I was and my father's criticism associated with food and weight manifested in me as constant worrying about how I looked, who accepted me, how much I weighed, and what I was eating. I assumed at a very deep level that there was something wrong with me. I would not let myself enjoy food without talking about how fat it was going to make me, or I would eat with feelings of guilt and shame. I developed a negative self-body image, I judged myself as fat much of the time and believed I was overweight, and so the dieting began.

I believe the issue I had with my weight was two-fold. It also stemmed from cultural confusion when I started comparing myself to non-Indigenous high school adolescents. I had moved to the city to continue my education, and I lived in several neighbourhoods where there were very few Indigenous youth or young adults around. Hanging together for breaks in the high school parking lot, I would overhear some of the boys openly comparing the girls to one another through derogatory comments. I remember overhearing the guys comment on how thin one of the girls was and this is what they preferred, or one would say, "Well, I like them thin and blonde." I knew I was neither thin nor blonde!

Of course, as a young teenager, I wanted to be liked and to fit in. This is normal adolescent sentiment as is feeling "awkward." As males age, and if this behaviour goes unchallenged, they can become righteous in their male privilege and domination. I learned much later that this is what can contribute to and cause patriarchy and misogyny. I believe many heterosexual males are unaware of the privilege they carry in their male gender. Instead of brushing off my negative experiences with teenage boys as a reflection of their stupidity and ignorance or copycat behaviour, I internalized their crude behaviour. I would look in the mirror and I did not see a girl who was thin and blonde. My feelings turned to shame and self-loathing.

My fears and worries about not being good enough, White enough, or thin enough became entrenched within me. My awkward, fear-based, low self-esteem also came from my family of origin. I realize that messages about body image were transmitted from my father, and I have no idea where he learned them from. My father continued to speak of how being thin was healthier or better, and he would constantly harp on this topic. I heard what he was saying and internalized that I was "fat" and "not good enough as I was."

My dieting journey probably started when I was about twelve years old. As soon as I could figure out a way to pay for a membership in Weight Watchers, I became a member. I have lost and gained the same thirty pounds several times through many years.

But, in my early twenties, I went to my first workshop on self-esteem and became aware of what I was doing to myself and how much I didn't like who I was. I decided to practice some of the techniques that were offered, such as positive affirmations and learning to love myself. Afterward, I realized I wanted to focus more on learning how to increase my self-esteem. My ongoing dieting and worrying about how I looked and how fat I felt did not end easily or quickly, but what did happen was a slow and steady progression of deepening my self-awareness, self-acceptance, and self-love. By the time I decided to quit the dieting and being an off-and-on-again member of Weight Watchers, I could not eat another tuna sandwich! I did not even like tuna, but I had forced myself to eat certain foods just to try and be thin. There was no joy or self-love in these moments; there was only a conviction that I had to be different and better than who I was, because I felt I was not good enough as I was.

Then one day, I stumbled across a wonderful book, *The Only Diet There Is* by Sondra Ray (1981).[2] I think this book is marvelous because it discusses how low self-esteem and negative thinking are associated with weight issues. I did all the suggested exercises and answered the questions as honestly as I could. By the end of it, I felt more connected to myself. I knew my self-love and acceptance had increased, and I decided to get off the dieting merry-go-round. Instead of dieting, I would access more therapy if necessary and continue forward on my self-love journey.

Ray's book taught me about forgiveness, spirituality, and positive affirmations to clear the past and create new possibilities for the way I felt about myself. I now have learned to reframe this obsession with food, weight, and body image as a journey toward healthier outcomes for myself. I am an older woman now and have become aware of what foods my body responds to more positively and what makes me feel unwell. I try now to eat mindfully and let myself choose what I want to eat and take responsibility for what I do eat.

But I also recall during the years I lived at home and within our community in my twenties that others accepted me for who I was, and I didn't feel judged about my body size or the size of my appetite. If I wanted to eat two baked potatoes at a meal, it was totally fine. I picked up on this acceptance and I felt happy about it. The generosity of giving and sharing food is an Indigenous cultural value.

As part of trying to fit in during my teenage years and as a coping mechanism, I started to consume alcohol, which made me feel more relaxed and part of the crowd. It gave me a larger sense of belonging, more self-assurance, and confidence. Feelings of inadequacy, low self-esteem, abandonment, and self-doubt all began to subside when I started to use alcohol. I began to turn toward it whenever I had the chance. I became a binge drinker and drug user most often on the weekends. The alcohol and drugs helped me to relax and have some fun with my friends. Hanging out with my friends was my favourite thing to do, which was normal adolescent behaviour. However, my alcohol and substance use in the quantity I was consuming was not normal. I used alcohol and drugs in binges regularly for many years, and I also became a workaholic. Workaholism at least seemed an acceptable trait. So, I worked hard and partied hard, and this became my lifestyle.

> I am brown and beautiful. My body is the perfect size and shape.

The routine use of alcohol and drugs continued throughout my youth and into adulthood. I would often talk with my dad about how sad I was feeling, or he would notice I was acting differently, or looking exceptionally sad. He suggested I speak with a counsellor; I knew my mood swings overwhelmed him and he worried. He also worried about my marijuana use and talked with me about it being a "gateway to more," that over time I would not find its effect enough, and it would cause me to look for harder drugs. I must give him credit for this talk and admit he was right—over time, I did want harder drugs. Yet, my binge drinking seemed acceptable, and Dad just put a sign over our washroom toilet with a symbol that indicated "no puking," and this was for me.

Journal Space: What are your coping mechanisms? Do you see them as healthy or unhealthy in how they affect your life? Take some time to honour yourself and your story and write what it means to you.

My experience was no different than what the literature speaks to about the effects of colonialism; I was plagued by low self-esteem. I had experienced suicidal thoughts and feelings, especially when I was under the influence of alcohol and drugs. I'm sure I could easily have been diagnosed as having a mood disorder. I had episodes of depression and issues with substance use in my past. I knew I felt so unworthy and constantly compared myself to others and, somehow, these comparisons were fixated on the negative. Remember, I felt not enough—not pretty enough, White enough, Indigenous enough, or smart enough. I had become consistently hard on myself in my self-perception.

There were traumatic situations experienced by my family members or within the community that also affected me, such as instances of family violence, or major disasters, such as fires, accidental deaths, deaths by suicide, and conflict. There were situational stressors that I internalized because I was part of a family, a community, and the collective. I would often go through bouts of depression or days with low moods, especially in my adolescence. I had difficulty relaxing when I was with others, and I wanted to control everything and everyone who did anything that increased my anxiety levels. Trying to control helped me feel safe, so I ended up living on my own while in high school at the age of sixteen years. Yet I often wanted a friend to sleep over or to come and stay with me. I constantly felt lonely and at various times I took in different roommates to live with me. It took me five years to complete high school because I developed a pattern of quitting and going back home.

There were days I struggled to get out of bed to go to school; I missed many days of school at this point in life. I was often either sick from the "brown bottle flu" (hungover) or feeling so depressed and lonely, I could not get out of bed or off the couch on Mondays and Fridays. Often, I would only attend classes Tuesday, Wednesday, and Thursday. I would write myself notes for the school office to explain why I was not in class. Then one day I was called down to the office over the intercom system, "Annette Alix, please come to the front office." I could not believe what I heard. I just wanted to crawl under my desk at that moment or completely disappear. I felt this large lump in my throat and the tears welled up in my eyes. I knew I was busted. I stood and walked out the door of my classroom and started making that long walk down the hallway to the front office. My mind was racing, wondering if I was going to get kicked out of school and have to go home.

The principal was waiting for me and took me into his office. He said, "Annette, we've noticed your attendance has been very poor and your notes have stated you have not been in class because someone has died in your family—your uncle, your grandmother, your cousin, and others from your community. Annette, I have to say, one person cannot be experiencing so much death at one time. What is really going on with you?" The sad truth for some Indigenous Peoples is that there are instances where this many people in their family do die, or multiple people within the community die, and there is no chance to catch one's breath to process the collective grief that occurs. However, this was not the case for me at this time—I was just making up excuses to try to cover up my absences. The principal knew I was living on my own and strongly suggested I see the guidance counsellor. I finally agreed and learned to let her support me emotionally. This counsellor became a champion for me; she took a vested interest in establishing a relationship with me.

I also had a teacher who was supportive, and I became her "hook up" for pickerel. I would make the arrangements to have the fish sent to me from back home. I would sell her the pickerel at a good price. It was a good relationship, a win-win for us both, and I let down my defenses and allowed her to help me help myself. Due to my issue with attendance, I agreed to go to her class after the school day was done and she would lock me in there—with my permission, of course—to work on different assignments I knew would not get done if I went home. Often, she would be in the room doing her prep work for the next day. We wouldn't say much to one another. I just felt safe and cared for knowing she was in the room, and I was not alone.

Even though my dad did not like school or have much connection to school, whenever I quit, he would encourage me to go back and try again. He would talk with me and listen to all my reasons for not wanting to be there and then he would send me back to try again. I loved learning, but my deep sense of disconnect made me feel like I did not belong at school. Dad instilled in me that there was no shame in trying and failing; what was not an option was quitting unless I was ready to go to work. Being young, I chose school as the easier way. I had tried doing a waitressing job for a short stint and the hours were long into the night, the customers were often rude and cranky, and I had no patience for the work. I was often being called into my boss's office for "my attitude toward the customers." It just wasn't a good fit for me. I knew I did not want full-time work at that point in my life. So, I did not give up on high school. I pushed down the shame and loneliness that haunted me, and I kept going and kept trying.

Although I didn't have the word *decolonization* in my vocabulary or any understanding of what it meant until I attended university in my thirties, my experience of decolonizing myself began in my twenties when I was struggling with alcohol and substance use, and my sister took me to my first Sweat Lodge ceremony. I had just finished another weekend of binge drinking and I was feeling so ill, it felt like I was going to die. I gladly accepted the offer from my sister to attend this ceremony. I knew I needed help for my binge drinking. I did not grow up knowing about the Sweat Lodge ceremony, but the Elders did not judge me. They took me in and cared for me in this ceremony. I accepted their help and was open to learning. I remember this ceremony was so cleansing and healing. It prompted me to start looking at why I was using alcohol and other substances to cope. It gave me strength to continue forward in my life. But I must admit, I was not cured of my behaviour; this took time and a few more "bottoms" as they say in recovery groups.

My choice to walk a life of sobriety at age thirty-two was one of the main reasons I decided to leave my home community and my family's business. At first, I was able to find support in my community from others who had experience with sobriety. I will never forget this kindness, friendship, and compassion shown to me. But after a year of staying sober in my community, I wanted and needed to find access to other resources. I felt like I was going to go back to my binge drinking behaviours unless I left. I needed to get help for myself as I now had a three-year-old son, and I had come to the realization that I needed to leave the relationship I had with his father. I had fallen in love with him while I was attending college in my middle twenties. We had met through mutual friends. He was a young Métis man and a gifted athlete. We had spent over ten years together, but I felt we were doing more harm to one another by continuing the relationship. I was completely falling apart.

In hindsight, I now believe I experienced a breakdown. I felt physically, mentally, emotionally, and spiritually exhausted. I remember I started crying and I could not stop. I called my brother and told him I couldn't make it to work. I was scared to stay home alone because I was feeling suicidal. I decided to phone a friend and asked her to come and be with me. She stayed for hours, listening to me cry as I told her what I was feeling. I was distraught for three days. I finally concluded that moving was the next right decision. I phoned my aunt and told her what I was going through, and she agreed to come and stay with me and my son while I prepared to move. I also had a dream of attending university. I got honest with my brother, father, and my son's father about moving and letting go of working full time in our family business. Even though these were emotionally difficult choices to make, I had to make them and follow through.

I didn't understand the options I'd had right within my community. In hindsight, I could have taken a leave from my work in the family business to go to a treatment program for my addictions, or I could have applied to university programs that were connected to my community. But this is not how my story went.

South – Cultural Reclamation, Understanding, and Self-Determination

My journey into cultural reclamation and the understanding of the history of colonization assisted me to move forward in integrating my spirit and healing my woundedness. I use the direction of the South here to locate me in the context of two key aspects. Some of my stories will relate to my youth but will also connect to the physical location from how I moved to the city which was south of where my community was. There, I continued forward on my healing journey with my education. Learning to incorporate the knowledge of both cultural perspectives and the formal education I was completing assisted me in my pursuit of wholeness and balance. I was moving forward and continually becoming stronger in my own self-determination.

Attending college with my peers gave me a group to belong with and a real sense of community. Yet, it wasn't until I learned more about colonialism and Indigenous teachings about the Medicine Wheel that

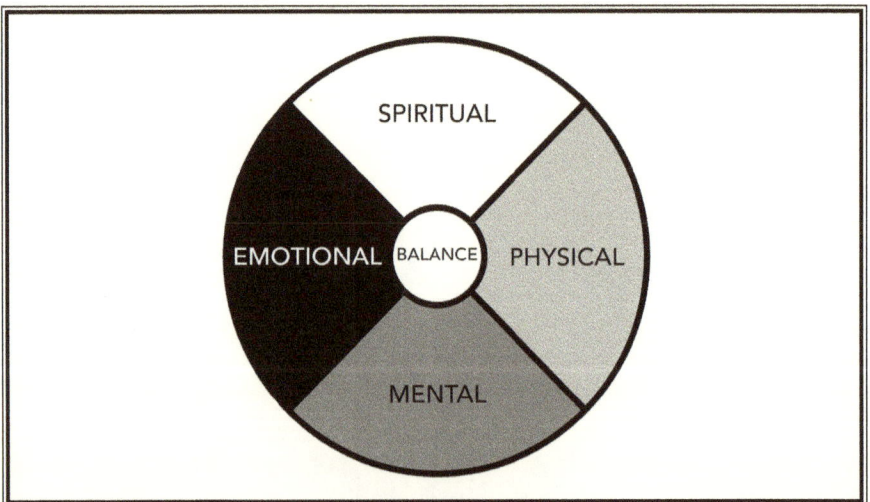

The Medicine Wheel

I began to go deeper in my own self-reflection, healing, and self-determination. I place the Medicine Wheel here to begin this section to provide a visual for how my life and story evolved.

I first began to learn more about being an Indigenous person in my years at college while studying Business Administration. At this point in history, Aboriginal was the word most in use to name who we were. I was part of a program that was specifically designed to support Aboriginal students in post-secondary education. This was an excellent opportunity where I was with other Aboriginal students like me, and I had access to financial subsidy (physical), support for tutoring (mental), and counselling (emotional). However, this was in the 1980s and the cultural aspects of this program were not yet created so there wasn't an opportunity to learn about ceremony and other traditional Indigenous teachings (spiritual).

Later, when I attended university, my learning expanded to many different topics, such as colonization, social determinants of health, classism, and racism. I pursued a Bachelor of Arts in Conflict Resolution, which was a faculty and program administered by Mennonites. Declaring conflict resolution as my major was a perfect fit at this point; it felt like I was attending free therapy while taking my courses. My courses in conflict resolution put me into classes and readings which discussed all aspects of conflict, such as intrapersonal, systemic, cultural, and international. There was also the opportunity to study the concepts of mediation. The courses I took in this faculty had the expectation for students to look within through self-reflection and learn to understand themselves more clearly. I recall the famous quote by Paulo Freire, "critical reflection is also action." I bought the t-shirt from the university store, and I wore it often as I learned and developed my own understandings and how to voice my opinions.

One day I was sitting on the grass outside of the university taking a break between classes. It was a hot day, the birds were chirping in the trees, and several students were sitting on other green spaces out in the university front yard. I was approached by a young, White woman who came directly toward me and asked, "May I sit here with you?"

"Sure, no problem," I replied.

We shared our names with one another, and her name was Rachel. Rachel began to tell me she was Mennonite and she said, "I am confused about my cultural identity being Mennonite. I am feeling lost because I am not particularly interested in living the expectations of a Mennonite life. This has caused me so much personal confusion and conflict with my family because I want to live differently than what they expect of me." She shared with me that she sensed I was feeling a similar way and was possibly confused about my cultural identity as an Aboriginal woman.

Rachel was right. I was feeling so lost and alone. I said, "Rachel, I am confused about who I am and how I am feeling at this time about my First Nations and mixed-blood identity and what I have been learning about colonization."

"I had thought so," Rachel said, "and even though I am White and Mennonite, and you are Aboriginal, I wanted to take a chance to connect with you and tell you about a book about your culture I know of."

The book was titled *The Sacred Tree: Reflections on Native Spirituality.*[3] Rachel's book suggestion was exactly what I needed and was how I found my first real connection to some of the teachings, beliefs, and values of my culture, again in written form, because this reality and information was not part of my life growing up. This book became my first connection to learning about the Medicine Wheel teachings and it became a guide for me, and I have used it for many years.

The Medicine Wheel is made up of a circle with four parts: the physical, mental, emotional, and spiritual. In its most basic form, the teaching is for one to work toward being in balance or living in harmony in their lives in the four parts of their Medicine Wheel. Alternatively, another way to think about this is that one can review the various aspects of their life, and it will help to show if one is out of balance in their life. Through this personal reflection, the realization and understanding can arise and with this self-knowledge, decisions can be made on how to proceed.

For example, I would look within at my Medicine Wheel in the four areas of the physical, mental, emotional, and spiritual, and I would realize I had not given enough time and attention to my son because I had been studying too much or too long on certain days. So then I would make time to nurture him and his needs. I would make the time to play with him and let him know how much I valued and appreciated and loved him. Once he was asleep for the night, I would continue with my studies.

If neglect or avoidance continues, this might cause a person to become out of balance or out of harmony. This imbalance may manifest in various negative ways in their life, or it may reveal to them where they feel lack or loss.

The substance use I was struggling with began in my youth and fit into the Medicine Wheel. My addictions affected all four areas of my

Medicine Wheel and created an imbalance and disharmony in my life. I was often not present in my relationships because I was focused on thinking about alcohol or drug use. I was also lying to myself because I didn't think I had a problem; it was everyone else's fault for how I had been feeling and behaving. Despite using substances as a coping mechanism, I did not understand what other options I had, nor did I understand when my trauma was overwhelming my reality. I did not understand that the colonization and systemic oppression I had internalized had created my cultural shame and confusion. This increased my susceptibility to use alcohol and drugs as a coping behaviour to help hide the shame and confusion.

The reality is that addiction becomes worse over time if it is not dealt with. It can have negative effect in all areas of our lives—personal, familial, communal, and especially our own mental well-being. I know this is how my addiction affected me. We can forget we are hurting ourselves when being caught up in the throes of addiction. Yet, it is often a common and readily acceptable coping mechanism for many until positive behaviours are learned and healthier choices are made.

My choice to pursue a Bachelor of Social Work degree was the beginning of a different level of healing for me. It was quite by accident that I even decided to go to the School of Social Work. I was a single mom and I thought I needed to have more than an Arts degree to secure a career which would give me the financial means to support me and my son. A friend of mine told me about Social Work and suggested I apply. He told me there were many opportunities in the field of Social Work and a need for more Aboriginal social workers and it was also a good path to be on if I was to pursue the goal of becoming a therapist. So, I did, and I was accepted.

I recall when I completed an assignment using a Medicine Wheel framework for an assignment in my Bachelor of Social Work, it was like a coming-out process in understanding myself more fully as an Indigenous person. I was learning about these teachings of the Medicine Wheel and defining myself and my story within it. It was a special time and healing experience.

This Social Work education also enabled me to learn about systemic oppression, colonization, structural social work, and advocacy. It was years later in my career that I chose the responsibility toward creating structural changes within bureaucracy. I focused on changing structural settings to enhance Indigenous knowledge and to respect and understand our Indigenous ways of being. My goal was to increase cultural competency and culturally relevant services in public, private, secondary, and post-secondary settings as well as healthcare. I became an advocate for the mental health of Indigenous people because of my Indigenous identity. I worked with some great colleagues—both Indigenous and non-Indigenous—to make some structural changes, but it was slow and sometimes grueling work. And now I realize this work I was doing was still within the colonial institutional structures.

Lavallee, B., & Clearsky, L. (2006) wrote "From woundedness to resilience: A critical review from an Aboriginal perspective" to address how systemic oppression has affected the overall health of Aboriginal people in urban centres. These authors challenge the reader to think about how colonization and assimilation have affected Indigenous people's health and well-being. They ask the reader to consider the concept of "woundedness" (p. 5) as another tactic of colonization that blames the Indigenous person, family, or community for their illnesses instead of laying the rightful blame on the systemic influences which continue to oppress Indigenous Peoples on an ongoing basis. Lavallee and Clearsky clearly address the socio-economic structural oppressive systems created through colonialism. Indigenous Peoples do not "choose to become diabetic nor do Aboriginal mothers wish alcoholism and early deaths on their children" (p. 5). The authors also advocate that continued practices of systemic oppression and marginalization are associated with large numbers of suicide amongst young Indigenous Peoples. The authors also state "some of our young people continue to commit suicide rather than live in a world that systematically denies their very existence" (p. 5). They argue it is critical for Indigenous Peoples to be treated respectfully and appropriately and argue for the concept of self-determination.[4]

> I can become emotionally dysregulated from reminders that I have been assimilated into the mainstream world through colonization.

The concept of self-determination must be included in the discourse on resiliency. It is through political, collective, and personal resistance to the ongoing colonial status and continuation of assimilation that Indigenous Peoples can find strength and thus self-determination. Consistent resistance to colonial practices is inherent to furthering Indigenous wholeness and cultural pride, and those working with Indigenous Peoples need to be aware of this reality. Lavallee and Clearsky recommend the need for spaces to be created where Indigenous Peoples can share their stories, be listened to respectfully, and free themselves from the historical and contemporary colonial structures that have hurt and hindered their overall well-being.

Research by Heilbron and Guttmann (2000) in the article "Traditional healing methods with First Nations women in group counselling" provides evidence for the use of Indigenous healing ways in group work practice. Their research emphasizes how incorporating Indigenous healing practices such as the "healing circle" (p. 7) gives Indigenous participants a culturally respectful opportunity to come together in a group to focus on healing from childhood sexual abuse. This study focused on combining the therapeutic modality of cognitive behavioural therapy and using the healing circle within a group intervention.[5] This form of engagement with the group of women was supported by evidence that First Nations women generally feel more comfortable gathering in groups as compared to individual sessions. The group process supports collective cultural norms as Indigenous ways of being, in that Indigenous people often feel more comfortable within community gatherings and collective settings when doing personal healing.

The women who participated in this study experienced the group intervention as a supportive, safe place and identified with each other as *Survivors* of past child abuse. They were able to share their feelings with one another about their past abuse because there was an understanding that other members in the circle had similar experiences. Heilbron and Guttman recommended the use of cognitive behavioural therapy techniques that could serve as a method to help the women learn to think differently about themselves in support of their healing from negative childhood traumas. Cognitive behavioural therapy was suitable because it was identified as "less culturally biased than other therapies" (p. 7) and it focused on the present moment in connection to what individuals are experiencing and thinking. Therefore, cognitive behavioural therapy is one way to change how we think, and I have found this therapy helpful in my own life too.

I easily identified with this piece of research by Heilbron and Guttman (2000) because I had been incorporating Indigenous history, aspects of my Indigenous identity, and non-Indigenous ways of healing as a natural part of my healing process. I had overcome my feelings of inadequacy and felt comfort in healing circles with other women. I learned to love all of me—the Indigenous and assimilated aspects of myself as I moved forward.

Overcoming Fear and Feelings of Lingering Inadequacy

I take you now to parts of my story that discuss the emotion of fear. I put the emotion of fear here in my story because I had a lot of fear to overcome which can be connected to my past and my internalized cultural oppression. My fears often fuelled my addiction. I think many people feel all forms of fear and often don't discuss it. I learned to mask my fear, stuff my fear, and let it paralyze me in some instances from moving forward with dreams and goals I wanted to pursue in my life.

Because fear is a common human emotion, it needs to be dealt with to lessen its power or alternatively to be used in a positive way. Fear can be a major block to living and trying to accomplish different tasks in life or to make attempts to complete any dreams and goals. I have had long talks with others about this emotion called fear. The emotion of fear can be perceived as real or imagined. This is the challenge to overcome and understand about fear. I had to learn how to feel my fear and continue to work toward my goals, dreams, and changes I wanted to make within myself and my life. I had to learn to feel the fear and still move forward, to go for it! When I have shared with someone, or wrote in my journal, or told my Creator/God, that I am feeling fearful, I have found the inner strength to persevere. I have experienced my fear subside; when I bring it out into the light, it generally dissipates.

When I was in high school, I had a kind teacher who tried to convince me to not quit a course with which I was really struggling. He asked me to stay in the course although my failure in it would be inevitable. He suggested I accept the failure and then take the course a second time. He tried to have me understand that despite failing it the first time, I was still learning something, and it was not a waste of my time. I did not listen, and I asked to be put into a different course I knew I would be able to pass. Many years later I understood what he was trying to do, and I regret that decision because my perfectionism and fear of failure continued to haunt me. I think, in hindsight, if I would have listened to this teacher it would have really helped me to heal this issue and I could have had access to other educational opportunities.

However, my high school experience and this hindsight did give me the wisdom to know it is important to periodically take more than one attempt in life to complete a goal. It took years for me, in some instances, to heal those old wounds of not feeling good enough or smart enough

44

and not being worthy or not realizing I deserved better. I think many people feel this way but keep their feelings hidden, deeply stuffed inside of themselves until provoked. Over the years, I have often said out loud some feelings or thoughts like this, and once I offered this sharing, others would agree and say, "Yes, I felt this way in the past," or "I feel like this right now." It is as though permission is necessary to show vulnerability. My experience with this emotion of fear rears its ugly head from time to time, and in each instance, I need to pause and understand what I need to do to overcome it. I need to recognize that maybe the simple answer is to practice more faithfully and routinely what it is I am trying to learn or change, instead of just thinking about it. I was surprised how—after many years of attending and completing different courses and degrees—fear surfaced when I was in graduate school.

This brings me to the story of one of the mandatory courses in my graduate studies program called Advanced Group Dynamics. The expected outcomes of this course were to create a group process, design and write the manual for it and then deliver it twice with two separate groups of participants. The delivery of the group process would be videotaped, and feedback would be received in weekly meetings with the course instructor.

I had facilitated groups, taught in classrooms, counselled individuals, and even presented at national conferences many times before registering for this course. Yet, I was completely riddled with fear; somehow this course scared me! This was an exceedingly difficult course for me to complete due to my fears—real or imagined—and my feelings of low self-esteem and self-doubt became activated.

As a result, it took me three attempts to complete the course. I registered three times and withdrew twice, and the course outline completely overwhelmed me each time I registered for it. I had to do this course. I had no other choice; it was a mandatory course. I had to push through my fears and negative feelings to overcome the challenges because deep in my heart I wanted to complete this degree.

Challenges were everywhere during my second registration. The course was taught in the winter session from six to nine o'clock in the evening; there were no other options. This was especially difficult because I am a morning person. My best productivity is from early morning until about supper time. This is a life-long pattern for me and is part of my personality. Attending night classes really was tough for me.

During this time, my father's health was deteriorating, and my emotions were drained. I also felt I had to pass up great opportunities for leadership in Aboriginal Health. My struggle with decision-making reared its ugly head. I struggled to let myself make choices that I personally wanted to make. I was fearful of saying "yes" to competing for the leadership opportunities in Aboriginal Health because I was riddled with self-doubt and lacked confidence in competing for a new role. What if I competed and lost? What would this say about me? Or if I were the successful candidate, how would I be able to do a leadership role with what I saw as having many responsibilities and be present for what my dad needed? I couldn't wrap my head around who would help my dad and be there for him if it wasn't me.

I'd had a history of feeling torn between doing work that kept me in front-line positions of helping others and my desire to be in administrative leadership positions. I had this distorted perception that to be a good person I had to always help others over my own personal desires. I kept thinking that doing administrative leadership was not helping others enough and now I know this is untrue; it is just a different form of helping. Those from my culture whom I was in relationships with, and was interdependent with, would be happy for me in whatever I chose because I was practicing the teaching of self-determination. But as it was, I left Aboriginal Health and went to work as a social worker in the public school system. Eventually I moved to a half-time position in a mental health program in the same town where my father was living so I would be available for him when he needed me.

Adding to my challenges, my husband and I had moved north of Winnipeg, a two-hour drive one way from home to the university. After working all day, I would drive to the university, partake in a three-hour class, and then face the long drive back home. It was cold and dark, and this was compounded by my night myopia. I could not see the road half the time and would lean forward trying my best to keep my eyes on the line in the middle of the road. I would keep the temperature lower in my vehicle so I would not fall asleep. Often it would snow, and my headlights would reflect off the falling snow. The temperatures on average were minus 25 degrees Celsius. After several weeks of this, I could not maintain this schedule, and I withdrew the second time. I felt like such a failure; I just could not push through and do what I needed to do. I cried all the way home that night.

Six years had passed, and I was running out of the time allowed by the university to complete my master's program. I had received the dreaded letter from the university that if I did not finish my overall program by a certain date, I would not be able to at all. I was still terrified at the thought of taking the course. My back was against the wall. I had to either face my fears or give up on my dream of earning my master's degree.

I completed the registration for the third time. I remember my first day of class, I looked around the classroom and saw all my fellow students and how much younger than me they were. I quickly assessed that I could be my classmate's parent or kookum (grandmother). However, I didn't let this bother me. I tackled one assignment at a time to overcome the fear that was still lingering when I would look at all the assignments. I asked more questions, seeking clarification if I did not understand, and this really helped to calm my fears and apprehension.

By now, my dad was extremely ill. There were often days I quietly held my breath wondering if this was the day he would die. On the days I had to attend the class, I would leave directly from work, make the long drive through rush-hour traffic into the city, and arrive to class just in time. On the way to class, I would call my dad and do a quick check-in with him as this would give me a feeling of connection and comfort. He in turn would know I was thinking about him, and I would always tell him I loved him. After class, it was cold, dark, and much quieter. Often during the long drive home, I would either call my husband or a friend to help me stay awake and grounded.

Once I completed the course, my professor and classmates were so thrilled. On the last day of class, we all celebrated with shouts of joy as many of them knew the challenges I had faced. I was immensely proud of myself too. This experience showed me that I had inner strength and faith to overcome my fears. Dad was still alive, and I was able to share with him the good news of finishing this master's degree. He was happy for me, knowing I had finally completed this goal.

Journal Space: Can you relate to how your fears have influenced your choices in life? Have you had to make several attempts at a goal you wanted to achieve, or have you had the experience of quitting after your first attempt because you just did not feel good enough or smart enough, or you let fear overcome you? Take some time to honour yourself and your story and write what it means to you.

Reframing My Fears and Moving Forward

Overcoming my fears and completing the course that I responded to with such fear, I had to challenge my distorted thinking and reframe my thoughts. I began feeling it was an exciting opportunity to combine my research on Indigenous mental well-being, years of working as a clinical social worker in both education and health sectors, along with my own life experiences, and combine these for my assignment. With my Indigenous research in hand, I was excited to design and implement a group process for persons who culturally identified as Indigenous and were supporting loved ones experiencing challenges with their mental health and well-being, whether or not they had received a formal diagnosis of a mental illness by a physician or psychiatrist. I knew I had my own experiences with mental health struggles relative to my Indigenous research; so, by completing this assignment, and creating and designing a group process, it became a personal (subjective) and academic (objective) endeavour.

Relationships are important to me and my culture, so I was happy to have the support and guidance of my professor who had known me for years within my Faculty of Social Work and was able to calm my fears and answer my many questions. I continued discussions with my advisor on where I would do my final practicum and how I would structure the work and what it would be about. I was also able to meet with the director of the Canadian Mental Health Association (CMHA) of Manitoba and Winnipeg for a networking lunch. We had not seen each other for quite a few years, but as we caught up with one another it became clear that I would be able to do my final practicum at the CMHA.

I was excited and hopeful because due to my long-standing relationship with these two people I felt comfortable in this decision to do my final practicum at the CMHA. For Traditional Knowledge and support during this practicum experience, I spoke with my Elder to ask for her guidance and blessings on doing this work. I received full permission to move forward, and my Elder also agreed to attend one session in each of the groups to provide her cultural teachings with the participants in my group. The group members also agreed to this step.

The group project I designed and applied was named "The Journey into Mental Well-Being Supporting One Another." I facilitated the project twice with two different groups of participants. The two groups were made up of adult women who identified as Indigenous (First Nations, Métis peoples, and Non-Status). I want to acknowledge the strength and resiliency of these women and how they trusted one another, me, and the process we all embarked on. My mother was also a participant within the first group. This took negotiation with my advisor for my mom to attend because this was different from the Western colonial perspective where professionals and therapy groups are offered with facilitators and participants who are strangers to one another. In the Western worldview, one must remain objective to deliver services. I often felt like I was jumping back and forth between the two paradigms—the Western worldview and the Indigenous worldview—to complete this work.

The research by Heilbron and Guttman (2000) strengthened my choice that utilized methods of the Smudge Ceremony and Sharing Circle in my project. I used my self-determination to make the decision to design and deliver the project in this way.

The group met one night a week for eight weeks, and the topics we discussed were decided by the women. There was commonality in their discussions—both groups brought up topics relative to colonization, the history of Indian residential schools, loss of language and culture, fractured family dynamics, and challenges with mental health. The discussions and sharing amongst the women also included the ongoing challenges of living with anxiety, supporting family members living with a diagnosis of schizophrenia, addiction, or effects of past personal and collective trauma and intergenerational trauma from the legacy of the Indian residential schools and relational trauma and racism.

Those who are accustomed to being in a Sharing Circle easily connect with the medicines and share as they wish and can release the feelings and story they have been carrying. It is a sacred space to release one's burdens. The space in a Sharing Circle is for witnessing and healing together, and it is not a space to comment on each other's story when shared. If there is anything said within the ceremony that one identifies with and connects with or learns from when they are in the circle, then that is the way it is supposed to be.

At the start of each weekly session, I facilitated a Medicine Wheel worksheet check-in as filled out by the participants. Next, we had a brief discussion on self-care and what this personally meant for each of them, and then I would lead a Smudge Ceremony and Sharing Circle. Afterward we would end each session with food and connection with one another.

For the Medicine Wheel check-in, participants used a blank Medicine Wheel template to draw or write about where they were in their wheel. I wanted the wheel image to be blank so they would have the freedom to make it completely personal and depict what was occurring for them as individuals. We would go around in a circle format and each person would share where they were at in the moment during each session. This was a helpful way for participants to share what was happening in their lives at the present time.

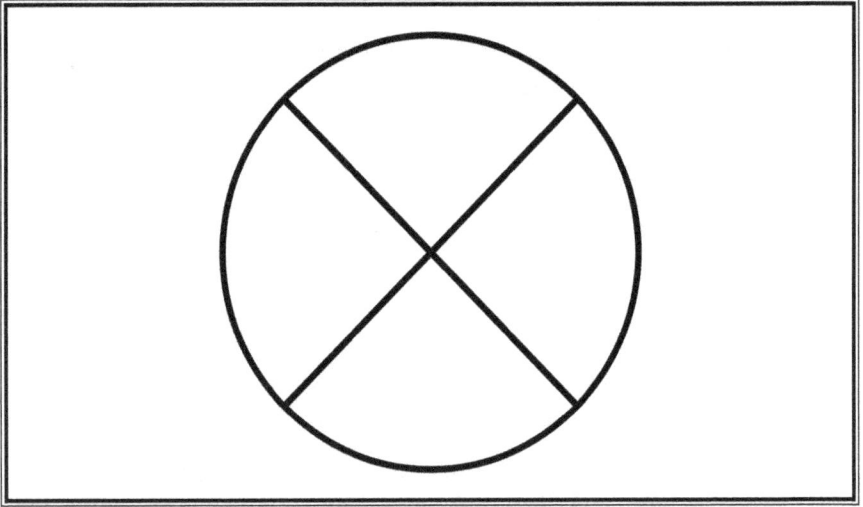

Blank Medicine Wheel template

Periodically, while I facilitated the group process, I would share some aspects of my story because of my experiences with similar issues affecting my mental well-being. In the Western world and professional therapeutic modalities of practice, this is called self-disclosure and is usually considered unprofessional.[6] From an Indigenous perspective, I was being real, sharing myself and how my mental well-being had been negatively affected by the history of colonization.

I explained this is how we heal as Indigenous people; we sit in the ceremony and share with one another. It is subjective, we are connected, and we support and witness one another's healing if those who are there agree to be there together for this healing connection. Everyone who participates in the ceremony receives their own specific insight and teaching. It is a collective process with individual revelations!

To facilitate my groups, I often used a small talking stick my son had made when he was in Grade 3. Using this talking stick with the participants kept me feeling close and connected to my son who is now an adult. I shared this story about my talking stick with the participants, and it was an opportunity to let them know a bit about me to support my connection to them. On most evenings when the group met, there would be tears shed and many different feelings to witness and process together. We would witness one another's pain, anger, and sorrow, and there was also a lot of laughter. We would end each session with the sharing of food and a time for relaxed connection with each other. I am forever grateful for the women who attended and allowed me the privilege to walk with them just for a moment in their journey, and to share in their stories and their personal healing. They taught me to believe in myself and to pursue goals and dreams that I had in my own life. They provided me with helpful feedback as participants about what was helpful and what was not. They supported me walking through personal fears of completing the course and my Master of Social Work program. I am forever grateful.

I also felt so supported in this process by having my mother there for the first group. She is a fluent speaker in our language, and she has many years of experience supporting others in their healing. She was also receptive to sharing parts of her story in the group. As the facilitator, I would often focus on the work I needed to be doing and was able to give her the necessary space to be who she is and share what was important in her life. She offered to cook bannock for the first group at the end of each of the eight sessions. She would drive over to stay at my house on the night before each session, make the bannock fresh each time, and then spend the night again after the session was over. The experience of having her with me in this journey also deepened my connection to her.

Yet, I was aware I was the graduate student, and I could not make the sessions about me, or more about me than the participants who were attending. I did the dance of balancing my own personal responses connected to Indigenous reality with the requirements necessary to successfully complete the course. The design I chose to use for the group when we

Upon completing this group process and receiving my graduate degree, I made a promise to myself that I would in some way share my own personal reflection on how the Indigenous research I completed intersected with me and my identity as an Indigenous, Ojibway, mixed-blood woman. I had managed to heal my own sense of woundedness. I wanted to create a culturally appropriate safe space for myself to process what I went through in my graduate work and in life because the research truly reflected aspects of my reality. My desire became this journal.

gathered was accepted as culturally appropriate and culturally respectful with those who were open and interested in participating in some of the traditional Indigenous ways of helping and healing, namely the Smudge Ceremony, the Sharing Circle, and the Medicine Wheel.

Healing Ceremonies

I now know and understand I am a colonized Indigenous person, but I have healed much of the pain that used to haunt and hurt me. This pain blocked me from loving myself and living in a joyful way.

The Medicine Wheel, Smudge Ceremony, Sharing Circle, Sweat Lodge, and powwow all support the healing and cultural identity of Indigenous people. I practice my spirituality with the Smudge Ceremony, and I attend powwows periodically and I am mindful of my Medicine Wheel of life. I have learned to say, "I am my culture, and it is not lost—I am."

I am continuously balancing my thoughts and feelings living in a bi-culturally socialized way. For example, while riding my bike, I might say my spiritual name and give thanks to Mother Earth and the Creator for my legs, the country road, the monarch butterfly, and the dragonfly that came to see me as I enjoy my time out in nature.

I have also realized that even though I like being with people and love others deeply, I have spent a lot of time on my own. There are layers of intergenerational trauma and emotional pain to walk through, and I cannot heal or change anyone else. I know this is true for me. What I can do is continue my journey in self-love and acceptance and continue with my own story. I can let myself grieve if I need; I can feel my emotions arising from any of my painful experiences, and I am able to learn new methods of grounding myself and believe in the new seasons of my life. I can reflect, realize, and accept this was how it was supposed to be.

> I live in a world where I have been raised and socialized in a bi-cultural way. I take from both the Indigenous and the Western worldview and use the teachings that I think and feel will support me the best. I am free to make my own decisions about this.

Medicine Wheel

In the context of Indigenous healing, the teachings from the Medicine Wheel are often used. The Medicine Wheel supports self-reflection, and if a person can locate themselves in their wheel and describe how they interpret their connection to the physical, mental, emotional, and spiritual parts of their lives and being, then they have a reference point on what they want to do. This is a culturally respectful way to assess where one is in their life through the process of self-awareness and self-reflection. Through the personal awareness process, one can use their location within the Medicine Wheel to figure out where they might want to make changes, what they enjoy, what relationships feed their spiritual well-being, or what is bringing too much negativity into their lives. Using the Medicine Wheel can be a form of self-determination. Most people find their situations are constantly changing depending on what is occurring in their life at each moment in each area of the physical, mental, emotional, and spiritual part of their wheel.

Learning about the Medicine Wheel in a manner I could understand helped me to feel supported as I unpacked my own life experiences. I began to understand my deep connection to the desire to find a sense of wholeness within me. I learned about interconnectedness and how everything is interrelated. I learned how important relationships are for me as an Indigenous woman. We are all interconnected to the land, animals, and inanimate objects. Just as the seasons change, people change. I knew I wanted to change and, indeed, I was changing. I knew that even though some of the change I desired would be emotionally painful, I was willing to make that sacrifice. The change I desired was worth it, and the goals I was creating were a part of the change. I learned about my spiritual self and the other three aspects (physical, mental, and emotional dimensions) of my Medicine Wheel.

During my Bachelor of Social Work degree, I experienced a growth spurt in the dimensions of my Medicine Wheel. My personal and spiritual development started to occur through dreams. I started paying attention to my sleep time and the dreams that came to me. For example, the symbolic representation within my dreams was there to guide me and provide information on how I was changing or what to change. I learned that my ancestors and people I loved who had transitioned into the spirit world would come to me in my dreams to offer their love and guidance or just to visit me. I started writing my dreams in a journal and would reflect on them whenever possible.

By this time, I had learned that if I thought I needed to seek advice, the Protocol was to offer tobacco to a spiritual Elder in a good and respectful way. I would offer tobacco to one of my trusted Elders and ask them for guidance and help for dream interpretation. Afterward, I could take my spiritual knowledge and understanding and share it with others. Once I understood what I was learning spiritually, I could take this knowledge and use it to choose my actions and make my decisions. All the aspects of my Medicine Wheel were activated. I made changes physically, I used my spiritual understanding, my mind, and my emotions to heal and grow my newfound sense of self. It was an extremely exciting time.

I am fully aware that the breadth and depth of the teachings of the Medicine Wheel are vast, and many Indigenous groups have different teachings within this perspective. It is beyond the scope of this journal to fully give the teachings of the Medicine Wheel the credit due. The point I am trying to make is that it is an Indigenous worldview and if someone wants to use it as a path to healing or a way to pursue their own self-awareness and self-determination, it can be used. The Appendix includes a list of questions to assist with the process of self-reflection. These questions can be starting points for deeper self-awareness and reflection.

Smudge Ceremony

The purpose of the Smudge Ceremony is to clear any negative energy a person may be holding within themselves or in the space around them, making space for positive energy. It is often used as a daily spiritual practice to connect with oneself and the Creator. This is a ceremony that is used by many and is common among ceremonies where people gather for the purpose of healing and meeting with one another. I use it often to help me feel grounded, or when I need to ask for specific prayers for others, or to give thanks for all my blessings. I have personally connected with this ceremony and use it regularly as a form of my spirituality in my life. It gives me great comfort and strength each time I make an offering of tobacco and use some of the medicines such as sage, sweet grass, or cedar to smudge and pray.

Sharing Circle

In the Sharing Circle ceremony, the Elder or facilitator of the ceremony informs or reminds participants of the teachings of equality in the circle. It is important to know the teaching of the circle: that everyone is seen and treated as equal in a circle ceremony. Everyone is safe and respected when in a circle ceremony. Sharing Circle Protocols may vary, but here are several I have learned: Participants are seated next to one another in a circle format. The Elder or facilitator of the circle will generally discuss the topic or reason for the Sharing Circle. There is often a Smudge bowl lit that is taken around the circle where participants can Smudge or touch the bowl or pass. Those who do not agree to Smudge can also wait until this part of the Circle is completed and enter the room afterward. There may be sacred items in the centre of the circle on a blanket on the floor, such as a copper cup of water (water symbolizes life), rattles, other medicines such as cedar, sage, or tobacco, or any other items the conductors of the Sharing Circle decide will be there. The leader of the circle will direct who will speak first.

Participants are encouraged to share or can pass if they decide they do not want to share. There is no talking while a participant is sharing. Those in attendance are there to witness and listen to what each participant is sharing. Once the Sharing Circle has started, it is protocol to remain seated in the circle until it is completed. It is a spiritual ceremony, so all in attendance agree with these teachings and behave respectfully and according to the Sharing Circle Protocols.

Sweat Lodge

I must make a disclaimer here that I know very little about the Sweat Lodge ceremony and give my utmost respect to the teachings and to those who hold the Indigenous Right and privilege to conduct it.

The Sweat Lodge is a dome-like construction made of willow trees, often covered by tarps or other natural materials. The four directions are represented in the Lodge. There is a doorway and a hole dug in the ground in its centre. Rocks are heated in a fire pit outside and close to the Sweat Lodge. I was taught that we call these rocks our Grandfathers or Grandmothers (depending on the conductor and lodge keeper) because they are part of our oldest living beings. When they are heated, they are brought into the Sweat Lodge and placed into the centre pit. The number of Grandfather rocks is decided by the conductor of the ceremony. I was taught that when I go into a Sweat Lodge ceremony, the lodge represents our mother's womb. The ceremony gives one a chance to be in the mother's womb again and to connect with the healing and comfort, to rebirth oneself in its healing powers.

There is direction for each different Sweat Lodge ceremony one attends. Generally, the conductor of the Sweat Lodge provides direction and Protocols to follow. When making the decision to attend a Sweat Lodge, it is expected that one will find out from others attending what the directions might be, such as what to wear, what to bring, or if there will be a feast afterward. Participants enter the Sweat Lodge and bring in their drums or rattles for songs that are sung during the ceremony when it is being conducted. The door is closed, it is very dark, and the heat rises in the lodge as water is poured over the Grandfathers. I attended a Sweat Lodge to receive my traditional Indigenous spiritual name, and I have also attended for my own healing as well as to support others.

Powwow

I did not grow up seeing or participating in a powwow gathering in my community. However, I have vague memories of my father telling me stories of what he witnessed about the traditional gatherings that would occur in Little Grand Rapids, MB when he was a child. This is many years ago as he was born in the middle 1930s. He told me stories of seeing big tents put up that were called wigwams. Families would come from other communities in canoes and set up their camps. They would cook and feast together and dance for several days. Big drums would be set up for the singers to use. It was a time of celebration and healing for those who attended. He told me he enjoyed sitting on the edge of the gatherings and taking it all in.

Besides learning about the powwow and traditional gatherings from my father, I had a girlfriend at my high school in the city who told me about the powwow and how she had a friend who was a dancer, and that this friend's whole family danced in the powwows. I was amazed by what I was hearing. At first, I was in disbelief—I couldn't believe that some Indigenous families were very familiar with the powwow and all danced. I wanted to learn more about their way of life. Yet, it took me many years before I found the courage to attend a powwow because of my own anxiety about not knowing what to do when I attended one.

Today, powwows generally happen over a period of one to four days, and dancers, singers, artists, and traders come from many miles away and from different provinces and from different states in the USA to dance. Spectators are made up of both Indigenous and non-Indigenous. Powwows are now generally grouped into two categories or divisions—a competitive (or contest) event and the traditional event for celebration or community healing.

As I became comfortable with my own Indigeneity and cultural understandings, I started to attend different powwows with friends and to watch family who danced. For example, I enjoyed going to powwows held in Winnipeg and by the time I graduated from my Bachelor of

Social Work, the University of Manitoba would host an annual pow-wow to celebrate and honour all the Indigenous graduates for the current year. This is one powwow I regularly attended for many years as it was such fun to see all the happiness of the graduates and their families. I also enjoyed seeing so many people I knew while sitting in the audience and observing all the singing, drumming, and dancing. I recall there was one year I counted thirteen drum groups, and I was overcome with joy to see the dancers in their beautiful regalia and to hear each drum group taking their turns singing.

There is generally a Master of Ceremonies at each powwow who coordinates which drum group sings and what type of dance will be performed. Many of the powwows are inclusive of spectators, and it is a wonderful time to go and join in from the audience. The powwow season generally begins in May and runs through the summer season. The number of powwows have continually increased over time and now there are even ones organized for dancing in the new year on either New Year's Eve or New Year's Day.

Journal Space: Do you have any practices you use to support your mental health and well-being to keep you in balance? Take time to honour yourself and your story and write what it means to you.

_____
_____
_____
_____
_____
_____
_____
_____
_____
_____
_____
_____
_____
_____
_____
_____
_____
_____
_____
_____
_____
_____
_____
_____
_____
_____
_____
_____
_____
_____
_____
_____
_____
_____
_____
_____
_____

Throughout my life I have often been there for many others—witnessing, supporting, and honouring their healing paths. This was special work and I feel very privileged and honoured to support others. When my masters work was completed, the realization came to me that I had to create a space to let my own voice come through and share how my research had affected me personally. I had been unable to do this while I was facilitating the groups and course work. But to help and heal myself, I needed to find a way to share how this Indigenous research and the work I was doing was completely relevant to me as an Indigenous person. This needed to be part of my journey to my own well-being.

I wanted to use my story relative to the research I had gathered and how I have worked to overcome the negative effects of colonization and how I am now able to be peaceful with who I am and how I interconnect with others and the various circles I find myself living in. This was my way of leaning into the teaching of: *you must learn to love yourself before you can love others*. I was raised in my culture to love others and to give to others, and now I have learned to give to myself, and this makes me whole and complete. This love is about sharing and caring for others and for me too. This is part of my self-determination. The writing of this memoir was my way of giving back to me. It was my way of bringing my story and academic work full circle.

Please feel free to draw or doodle anything that comes up for you. This is your memoir journal.

Journal Space: Can you relate to the experience of needing and wanting to find space for your own voice and healing? Take time to honour yourself and your story and write what it means to you. How do you love others and show love to yourself?

_____
_____
_____
_____
_____
_____
_____
_____
_____
_____
_____
_____
_____
_____
_____
_____
_____
_____
_____
_____
_____
_____
_____
_____
_____
_____
_____
_____
_____
_____
_____
_____
_____
_____
_____
_____

West – Becoming Balanced

As I learned more about my Indigenous culture, I understood that re-lationships are important for a sense of well-being and connection. Colonialism and how I had felt about myself as an Indigenous per-son affected how I experienced many of the different relationships I had within my family of origin, my friends, my community, and how I thought and felt about myself. Here I share different perspectives I had at various times and ages in my life and how I perceived them to be connected to my issues with abandonment, loneliness, addiction, grief, intergenerational trauma, and oppression. To this end, I embarked on my process of interpersonal decolonization and worked toward a new self-concept that feels peaceful for me. I became grounded in my own spirit and sense of self. This is why I have the direction of the West at the beginning of this section, as it signifies that I am an adult and can look within my Medicine Wheel and share parts of who I am with others and stay grounded and in balance as I relate with others. The west is where the sun sets, and peace—and acceptance of what is—can come when I witness a beautiful sunset.

Relationships and Connectedness

I attribute my attachment issues to colonialism for how it has affected my attachment to my family and my relationships with others. I under-stand that colonialism had intergenerational and interfamilial effects. I am only sharing how I saw things and situations in my family, but I know that colonialism affected everyone and our community. There are continual challenges to overcome in how I relate to others and how I feel and think they relate to me. It has taken continued effort to heal, rebuild, and sustain the threads of connectedness in relationships. In the most simplistic way, I have learned colonialism is based on individualism, industrialization, capitalism, and power over.

But, growing up in my family of origin, I did have memories of the teachings regarding generosity, caring, and sharing. I was taught about accountability and responsibility to one another as a family and community. It was also instilled in me to have respect for our Elders, nature, plants, and animals. This is a collectivist worldview; it is holistic, and relationships are reciprocal, interdependent, and important. For example, when meeting up with someone after a long time, we always ask with genuine interest after the well-being of our mothers, siblings, and many other questions about family, relatives, friends, or any others' well-being.

I have had to remind myself that—before colonization—our collective way of being was for individuals, families, communities, and nations to support one another. The Elders and older adults provided guidance, direction, and teachings necessary to help the younger ones learn the necessary roles and responsibilities to become confident, functioning adults. There was the understanding for the need to help one another and the values of generosity, caring, and sharing were instilled in everyone.

Everything is connected: myself, my spirit, the plants, animals, land—everything! When I care about something or someone, it has been hard for me to let go and let the relationship end. I used to judge myself for having such difficulties, but now this is an integral part of me that stems from my cultural spirit. When I experience relationships, they have life and value, and I can see and feel all the nuances and interconnectedness. My relationships are holistic, spiritual, and do not begin or end with me. I continually learn and grow with each circumstance and relationship I encounter.

Grandfather rock in shape of a heart

Relationships and the balance with self and others and connectedness are important to my well-being. I am a relational being. I come from a collective cultural background. I know I do my best when I have relationships with others in which I feel safe and comfortable. I am closer to living in balance when I interact with other people. Therefore, I share how being able to learn about Indigenous ways of healing and interacting with others was an opportunity to heal from the effects of colonization. It was a perfect fit for me to explore, design, and facilitate the practicum in my Master of Social Work program.

Journal Space: What are your thoughts and feelings about the relationships in your life? Have they been influenced by different worldviews or family expectations or affected by colonization? Take some time to reflect and to honour yourself and your story.

Perception: Abandonment, Loneliness and Sorrow

I have come to understand that the internal confusion and low self-esteem I have healed was caused by the organized, external, oppressive systems of colonization. I now proudly identify myself as woman of Ojibway descent, an Indigenous woman, and I acknowledge I was born into colonization. Because I learned about the process of decolonization in my formal education, I have since been decolonizing my mind and whole being over the last twenty-five years so I can feel proud about myself as an Indigenous person. I have worked to understand and reclaim and heal aspects of myself relative to my loss of cultural identity and knowledge. I accept who I am today and do my best to just "be" me. I have committed to letting go of the self-criticism as best I can. Many people have told me over and over that I am "too hard on myself." I am finally listening to these kind words of advice from others, and this is what I choose now, to be kind to myself as I try my best to be kind and compassionate to others. I give myself the permission to be happy, to focus on what is joyful in this life of mine.

Despite knowing both intellectually and spiritually that the intergenerational trauma of the systemic oppression of colonization experienced by my ancestors and my family created issues within me, I was left with this reality and the responsibility to find my way forward in healing myself, for my son, my family, and subsequent generations. I needed to find a way to stay alive—literally stay alive—because there were many times my moodiness and low self-esteem took me to those dark places of suicidal thoughts. I did not know how to handle my emotions, those low moods, and often my racing thoughts. This is the work I had to do, to learn how to live my life and manage my emotions. I did not know how to communicate without either being too passive (soft and meek just agreeing with everyone) or too aggressive (getting mad and yelling) when I was trying to share what I was feeling. Sometimes I would completely shut down, and I would want to run away, far away from everyone and everything.

Please feel free to draw or doodle anything that comes up for you. This is your memoir journal.

Journal Space: Can you relate to having struggles and challenges in managing your emotions? Take some time to honour yourself and your story and write what it means to you.

_____

_____

_____

_____

_____

_____

_____

_____

_____

_____

_____

_____

_____

_____

_____

_____

_____

_____

_____

_____

_____

_____

_____

_____

_____

_____

_____

_____

_____

_____

_____

_____

_____

_____

_____

Even as an adult, I continued to yearn for a deeper connection and relationship with my mom, but because of the geography of where we lived and the miles between us, it was an almost insurmountable challenge. Mom moved to various places in and out of Manitoba and later to British Columbia. We had an opportunity to connect when I was preparing to give birth to my child.

I was scared to give birth, but I know I loved the thought of being a mother. As soon as I became pregnant, I started thinking of the baby inside me and addressing everyone as though the baby were a separate person and we were one entity, or a team. For example, I would say "we are on our way" or "we are hungry/tired" or "we need to go for a walk." I loved being pregnant, and I would read to my belly and talk to my baby inside my womb.

I was in my eighth month of pregnancy and working approximately fifty to sixty hours per week managing our family business with my brother when my medivac occurred. I had started to experience increased blood pressure, and the doctor was concerned about the onset of gestational diabetes. I was sent into Winnipeg six weeks before my due date. Today I laugh about how no one even thought of me going on maternity leave. I came from such a workaholic family that we didn't even know it was an option.

My mom came from her home in British Columbia to be with me. She brought with her my sister's daughter who was nine months old. At first, I was frustrated with Mom bringing along my little niece, but then I quickly accepted that this is how things were done in our family. My child's father was in college and had rented a small suite in Winnipeg where we (Mom, little niece, me, and my child's father) all settled in together for my confinement. I was not allowed to go back to my home community until the baby was born. We made the best of it while all in this tiny little space. I remember I craved olives and banana cream pie through my pregnancy, and we had many evenings of sharing banana cream pie and tea together while we waited for baby to arrive!

Finally, the big day came, and we were in the hospital waiting for my baby to be born. Mom was sitting with me and began telling me stories about the land and the bush while I was having contractions, and it was driving me nuts. Mom had previous experience helping my sister give birth and she shared with me that my sister enjoyed the storytelling, but I had to ask her to stop talking and just help me walk around. She was surprised that I didn't find her storytelling soothing, but she quickly shifted gear and started walking with me. My niece had another caregiver that day, and I was glad to have my mom's full support.

As it turned out, I had to have a caesarean section to deliver my baby—a whopping nine-pound, fifteen-ounce boy. He was so long, the baby sleepers we had brought with us only came to his knees. We were so proud and happy. When I finally held my son in my arms with my mother sitting beside me, I looked over at her and I felt love, such unspeakable love that I had never imagined or felt before. I felt love for her, for me, for my new baby, and for my entire family. It was such a blessed moment. I was grateful Mom was so kind, thoughtful, and generous with her time.

Years later, during my healing journey, I had a thought that my mother may have been living with depression during her pregnancy with me. Because of how I so often felt sad as a child, I wondered if I had picked this up in utero. One day, my mom and I were sitting together at the kitchen table while drinking a cup of tea as we often do while we play her favourite game of cards called Bear Claw. We were home alone; the house was peaceful and quiet. Our old dog was laying on his bed inside the living room and our grouchy old cat was sleeping on the couch. I decided to ask my mom about what I had been thinking about this possibility of her feeling depressed when she was pregnant with me. Mom did not go into any detail about her pregnancy with me in this moment, but she did say she agreed with me about the possibility of her being depressed when she was pregnant. She also said, "You were such a good baby too; you didn't make much of a fuss and sometimes I think we might not have paid enough attention to you because of this. We were often working in the store, and we often had you under the counter in an orange box wrapped in blankets. We would check on you, but you did stay there for quite some time each day."

I finally felt validated after this discussion with my mother. It felt so good to know this wasn't a fabrication of my mind, but rather something my own intuition and spirit knew. I think it is a gift when there is an opportunity to sit and listen to one another and hear each other's perspectives and heal our threads of attachment to one another. This was a very healing moment for me. Another beautiful gesture Mom provided in my twenties was a birthday card in which she wrote about the day she went into labour with me. This was such a beautiful gift and card to receive. I still have that card, and I have pulled it out and read it time and again on other birthdays.

Journal Space: Have you ever had magical or healing moments where everything comes into alignment and you feel complete love, forgiveness, or understanding? Take some time to honour yourself and your story and write what it means to you.

Alcohol, Substance Abuse, and Workaholism

After years of living with the ongoing struggle with my moods, alcohol, and the drugs, I finally realized that I had to find ways to change my life and my negative thoughts. I felt so stuck; yet, I wanted to move forward, to live, and to achieve my goals and dreams. I felt especially suicidal under the influence of alcohol and other substances, which amplified my negative thoughts and feelings. This did not occur every time I used alcohol and drugs. But there were enough instances that, if I am honest, I easily could have completed suicide in a blackout or how (and I hate to admit this) when I had been driving under the influence, I could have easily killed myself or someone else. What a tragedy it would have been if I had done something so awful in a drunken stupor. I remember one hangover when I was so sick, I thought I was going to die. I called the nursing station to talk to someone for some help. I do not know who the nurse was on the other end, but they just said, "Quit your darn drinking, take some aspirin, go to bed, and sleep it off." The inappropriate roughness of the nurse's reply aside, there was absolute truth in what she told me.

At thirty-two years old, I finally made the decision to pursue a life without them (alcohol and drugs) and I chose complete abstinence. I say "them" when I describe alcohol and drugs because it is as though the substances had a life of their own and created the illusion that they were my friends and that I couldn't live without them. Although I knew I was harming myself, there was also fear in letting them go. I had this idea in my mind that an alcoholic was someone who drank every day. I didn't think it applied to someone who drank only on the weekends or certain occasions, even if they would overdrink and become completely intoxicated.

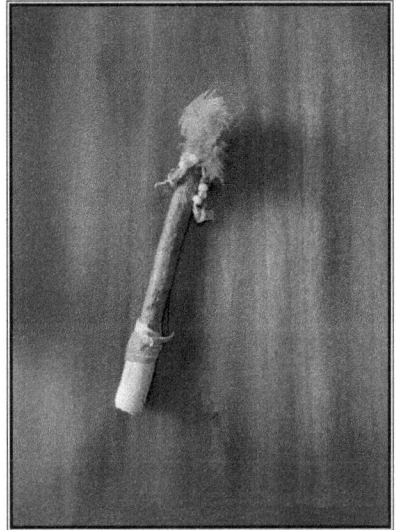

Talking stick made by my son in Grade 3

To get started in my journey of recovery, I reached out to a relative who I had witnessed changing their life. I asked them how they did it, and I was given the information and compassion I needed. I believe my self-determination journey was important because I had a three-year-old son who needed me to live and to be a healthy, happy parent. I genuinely wanted to be alive and well for him. I knew deep in my heart that I wanted change in my life, and I knew I had the power to change myself, but I still did not feel any love for myself. The love I felt for my son was the reason I started my recovery journey.

When I started my healing work, I found help in twelve-step meetings. This was where I began to look at my behaviour and my coping mechanisms. I learned more positive, new ways of coping. I learned how to let go of the troubling behaviours and continued to follow a program of recovery. I learned how to live life sober and to be present to my feelings.

I started healing the relationships in my life and taking responsibility for the quality of them and my part in them. I worked on completing the twelve steps with guidance from a trusted helper. I learned how I could start making amends to people I had hurt, and I followed the steps to heal important relationships in my life. I stopped blaming my family and others and I started taking ownership of how I was feeling and behaving in my relationships and situations in my life.

During this phase, I still believed I could change others. I tried hard to get others as excited about recovery as I was, and I quickly learned it was not possible. What I did learn was that I had no control over what others said and did, and it was not my job to tell them what I thought they needed to do or how to live their lives. I learned to focus on my own mental health and well-being. I began to learn to trust myself and my own spirit.

It was not an easy journey, but the longer I stayed sober and committed to a sober way of life, the better I started to feel about myself and my life. I learned to trust myself and to make decisions that worked for me. My mood began to stabilize, and I started to feel hopeful and healthy. I felt stronger and happier as the days turned into years. I learned to heal the painful emotions, and I stayed long enough on my recovery path that my self-love and acceptance eventually began to settle in and blossom.

It was not until many years later—after much of my own inner work, recovery, and healing—that I came to realize that my parents had done the best they could with what they had. In my own healing, I worked on forgiveness of myself, my parents, and others. It was my responsibility to focus on my own healing and recovery. As an adult, I own my feelings, and they are something I can work toward changing if I want to.

It took me many years to understand myself and walk through all the different issues I had internalized along the way including those associated with colonization. I could relate to what the twelve-step literature was saying, and I began to connect and realize where my issues and challenges had begun. The research I completed provided me with contextual validation for what has negatively affected my mental health and well-being. Now I had some external validation and understanding of where my cultural confusion and issues stemmed from.

At the time of publishing this memoir, I am grateful to say I now have over twenty-eight years of living free from alcohol and substance use. I live in sobriety "one day at a time" with the support and continued involvement with twelve-step groups. The work I did as a part of the twelve-step groups highlighted the challenge and responsibility of finding out how I could heal and how I could learn to feel better about myself and how I was choosing to live my life. Everyone is so different even if we are part of a cultural group, family, and community.

> Through cultural reclamation and continued use of the cultural ways and language, there is openness and strength occurring amongst families, people, and nations.

Please feel free to draw or doodle anything that comes up for you. This is your memoir journal.

Journal Space: Are you doing any inner work or participating in anything that is helping you to heal or discover or uncover answers for yourself? Take some time to honour yourself and your story and write what it means to you.

Understanding and Transition

Higher education and understanding the political landscape played key roles in my decolonization process. During my years at college and university, my educational interests often led me on a path toward searching for a deeper understanding of why humans behave the way they do and what root causes there are for some people to feel so negative about themselves. This higher educational experience gave me the opportunity to pursue the many answers I sought while I also learned about the history of Indigenous Peoples in Canada.

The political landscape in Canada was changing due to the cultural and political advocacy and strength of Indigenous leaders and grassroots people. Political and advocacy work had been going on for many years; however, I became aware of it only when I left home in the 1980s to attend college.

For example,

"The National Indian Brotherhood became the Assembly of First Nations in 1982, now representing 634 member chiefs across Canada. The Native Council of Canada (NCC), which formed in 1970, represented Métis and non-status Indians and pursued changes in government policies with respect to Aboriginal rights, economic development, education, and many other fields. In 1993, the NCC was reorganized and renamed the Congress of Aboriginal Peoples."[7]

These were exciting times for my generation. Grassroots organizations and political advocates had paved the way for higher education for Indigenous youth. In Manitoba, programs were created that provided support in academic, financial, and counselling programs. I want to say miigwech (thank you) to the people for their bravery to keep fighting for systemic and structural change. They gave so much to improve life for so many. Because of their hard work and sacrifices, I was able to pursue my degrees.

However, this was a complex reality because I had to leave our community to learn this historical information about colonization and its impacts on Indigenous Peoples. This was actually a barrier I had to overcome—I had to give up the safety and comfort of my current life and community to make this move. Although attending college was an exciting adventure, learning about the effects of colonization and the

Indian residential schools also created a grief response and sadness at the same time. I realized that I had lived in a real bubble in our community where everyone knew one another, and it felt safe. Despite my internalized confusion, my community was all I knew, and I did feel connected to it. I could look out my window and see my best friend's house or I could run up the road to a friend's or my cousin's home. From this perspective, life was amazingly simple.

When I initially attended Red River College at age nineteen, my internalized confusion followed me, and it influenced my decision-making process. I first enrolled in the Industrial Arts Teacher Education program. I wanted so badly to do something different for a career, to breakout on my own path other than becoming a teacher, nurse, or social worker. In hindsight, there is research I recall that acknowledges the reality of why so many Indigenous students became teachers, nurses, and social workers—it was due to these being the only professionals we saw in our communities as we grew up. There was no access to learning more about different job and career options in my community.

I struggled with my self-esteem and lack of confidence as I started the Industrial Arts Teacher Education program. I wanted to quit midway through the first term, but my dad encouraged me to finish the term and to not leave with bad feelings. He taught me that this was an opportunity to leave things in a good way and to not burn bridges, to be responsible even though I just wanted to run away. I followed through with his suggestion and finished the term before withdrawing from the program.

After working in our family business for several years, I returned to college and completed a certificate in Business Administration. I was still quite culturally confused and was identifying as Métis, just like my mother. One day while I was in college, I shared with another Indigenous classmate about my cultural confusion and he said, "I have no confusion about who I am. Every time I look in the mirror, I can see who I am, and I know who I am." He was a very funny, smart man with very dark skin and a great smile. I felt envious of how clear and concise he was about his identity. I was still unaware that what I was experiencing was internalized, self-cultural confusion.

Meanwhile, Indigenous Peoples were becoming increasingly aware of the oppression that was occurring in Canada and this awareness trickled into our community. Eventually, the national changes in Canada sparked by political advocacy, such as the patriation of the Canadian Constitution, Section 35 (1982) which recognized and affirmed Aboriginal Title and Treaty Rights. Then Section 37 was amended, which obligated the federal and provincial governments to consult with Indigenous Peoples on outstanding issues. Likewise, the amendment to the Indian Act to Restore Status (1985) occurred. Bill C-31 amended the Indian Act and changed how I would and could identify as an Indigenous woman.

My sister started to pursue a deeper understanding of our cultural identity. She shared her findings and became a cultural advocate and leader for justice and recognition for us as Indigenous women and people. Because of her pursuit of gathering the information on our Indigenous lineage, I was able to follow suit and apply to the Canadian government under Bill C-31 and claim Indian Status. In 1992, I officially became a member of Miimiiwiziibiing (Berens River First Nation), where I had grown up and—despite my challenges—felt connected. Acquiring Indigenous status was a huge step in the healing of wounds and overcoming the feeling of not belonging. I found it interesting that our mother applied for her membership to the Cowessess First Nation because her mother was from that community. Our grandmother was orphaned at five years old and raised by the grey nuns of the Marieval Indian residential school in Saskatchewan.

My passion and commitment to learning more about colonization and its effects on our mental well-being as Indigenous People fueled my resolve and helped maintain my focus while practicing as a clinical social worker later in my career. I continued to research topics such as suicidal ideation, trauma, post-traumatic stress, depression, and substance use. These factors are often noted as common mental health diagnoses for many who identify as Indigenous. I personally knew these topics were relevant and applicable to Indigenous mental health and well-being because I had experienced them in my own life and had witnessed and supported many others with similar struggles. Moreover, I also began to understand how these effects influenced subsequent generations. It is imperative to be conscious that the trauma and effects of the past are intergenerational and continue to be transmitted in present day. I have witnessed incarcerations, experienced multiple losses, and attended far too many funerals of completed suicides. I know the effects are real. The intergenerational effects of the Indian residential schools all make so much sense to me now.

Please feel free to draw or doodle anything that comes up for you. This is your memoir journal.

Journal Space: How are you feeling? Do you have any responses to this part of my story in your personal life or your chosen career and focus? Take some time to honour yourself and your story and write what it means to you.

One study by Elias et al. (2012)[8] explored the effects of the Indian residential school system and its relationship to the high suicide rates among the Indigenous population in Canada. A large sample size of data was gathered in 2002/2003 with 2,953 First Nations adults; 611 who had attended Indian residential school and 2,342 who had not. Elias et al. (2012) also focused on the trauma and suicidal behaviours on and off reserves for the participants in this study. They discovered a link to suicidal thoughts and behaviour for those who had attended Indian residential schools. Even the children of those who attended residential or day schools had a propensity for intergenerational effects as was demonstrated in their behaviours. These effects were identified as historical trauma, i.e., personal effects passed along from one generation to the next generation most often due to the loss of parental/sibling bonding, forms of physical, sexual, and emotional abuse, and years of enduring cultural shaming.

One could argue several important outcomes from the research showing that—for those living on reserves—females were more likely to have experienced levels of abuse, suicidal thoughts, and attempts at suicide. Likewise, a history of suicide attempts was more prevalent in younger populations with single males at higher risk for suicide whereas females experienced poorer mental health and higher levels of abuse when experiencing stress in their lives. Consequently, based on the results of this study, I agree that the experiences of Indigenous Peoples were not only historical but continue to this day.

Those who attended the residential schools experienced major assaults as individuals, families, and communities. The forced governmental policies were designed to eradicate cultural identity, familial and community bonds, and to Christianize the Indigenous students and assimilate them into the Canadian landscape and economy. The Indian residential school system continued into the mid-1990s and affected multiple generations. Indigenous Peoples lost connections to their land, each other, their languages, and familial ways. The effect of this cultural disconnection cannot be overstated. A review of history in the Canadian context and the process of colonization which occurred has solidified the Indian residential school experience as a major contributing factor to the demise of the mental well-being of Indigenous Peoples on every level.

Many Indigenous people chose—for mere survival—to adhere to the oppressor's rules and thus gave up their languages, cultural practices, and ways of being. Many Indigenous people felt lost and shamed for being Indigenous. They disassociated from their cultural identities and customs by refusing to speak their languages or practice their ceremonies, instead opting to become assimilated into Canadian society. Because of the pain and demoralizing experiences instigated by the colonizers and racist practices, many Indigenous people completely internalized the external oppressive experience while suffering trauma and—to cope—resorted to the use of alcohol or other substances, experienced suicidal ideation, and had low self-esteem.

Journal Space: Are there any memories or current behaviours or situations that are coming up for you? Take some time to honour yourself and your story and write what it means to you.

Intergenerational Oppression and Collective Grief

Bombay et al. (2014) argue that the concept of historical trauma and intergenerational effects is a contributing factor to increasing levels of depression, substance use, and suicidal behaviour within Indigenous populations. The challenge arises to consider how not only the individuals, families, and communities have been directly involved and have been affected, resulting in many living with hopelessness, anxiety, and suicidal ideation, but more importantly to be aware that the ongoing collective stressors and trauma that began in the past may be contributing to the overall demise of Indigenous health today.[9]

The structural implications of the history of the Indian residential schools are overlooked and result in diagnoses being transformed into individual pathological diagnoses in mental health and illness. Therefore, it is argued that the historical experiences of Indigenous Peoples in Canada need to be seen and understood within a collective and structural context of how the Indian residential schools were specifically created to eradicate Indigenous culture and ways of being. What is of greater significance is the experience of Indian residential schools and the historical traumatic effects that have resulted in an actual collective trauma experience that is intergenerational.

Remember that my parents were students at the day schools operated by the Catholic Church in our community. I believe their experiences in these schools affected how they raised me and how my sense of self was formed. They experienced their own levels of this historical trauma that the research speaks to. They could go home each night to their families, but the external influences of the church and state were ever present. It became normal not to talk about who we are as Indigenous People and there was a feeling of being ashamed that became prevalent. For example, my parents spoke the Saulteaux/Ojibwe language fluently, but I believe their fear that their children would experience racism stopped them from teaching it to us. These are my own personal thoughts. I have made several attempts to learn how to become a fluent speaker with little success. However, I keep trying. I do enjoy listening to others who are fluent Saulteaux/Ojibwe speakers. My heart fills up with love when I eavesdrop on our mother and auntie talking with each other in our language and there are instances when I can understand some of what they are saying. This is another aspect of myself I must love and accept as I try not to spiral into feeling "less than." The process of decolonizing myself can be exciting and tiring at the same time.

As a child in Miimiiwiziibiing (Berens River First Nation), I remember thinking that I was not an Indian because our family had running water and flush toilets in our home. I had confused culture and classism. Somehow, I internalized that I wasn't an Indian (this is what we were called back when I was a child) because of how I had access to infrastructure, such as running water, which my dad had worked to have available for us. Can you believe this—basing one's cultural belonging on whether you have access to sewer and water systems? How messed up was that!

> When I am triggered about not being able to speak my culture's language fluently, I remind myself I am worthy and loved the way I am and in how I do communicate. My ancestors know this, and my family, relatives, and friends love and support me.

What I know now is that structural forces of the colonial policies segregated Indigenous Peoples and forced them onto pieces of land, creating the reserve systems that contributed to the lack of infrastructure in communities. Miimiiwiziibiing (Berens River First Nation) still has water delivered by truck, and sewage is picked up and transported to a lagoon. Families also do not have access to sewer and water systems in their homes. There continues to be many reserves that are on advisories for potable water and do not have full access to sewer and water systems.

Miimiiwiziibiing (Berens River First Nation) was a small community and not much happened without everyone knowing about it or being affected by it, but I did not understand what was causing some of the pain and strife. I would see people experiencing situations of domestic violence or accidental deaths, and I had my own personal experiences with violence and anger that would rear its ugly head, especially when I was under the influence of alcohol. It seemed what I could not say or communicate when I was sober would periodically come out in angry outbursts when I was drunk. What I was really struggling with was my feelings. I did not know how to communicate what was going on inside of me in a healthy way.

It was especially challenging when I felt so much of the pain internally from what was going on externally around me. Witnessing or hearing about families in conflict had this effect on me. Compounding my pain were many situations where multiple losses had occurred by death or violence. Everyone experienced many instances of grief and loss, which became a "collective grief" that our community has consistently had to endure and overcome. Before a person or family or the community can move through a grief and loss process, another loss has occurred, creating a "cumulative grief."

For example, at one point in my years practicing as a clinical social worker, I knew at least twenty-five young people who had died by suicide, and I could not attend any more funerals of this type. The collective and cumulative grief was overwhelming, and I had to stop and take time to heal from how this affected me. This was difficult, but I had to choose to focus on my mental well-being. I felt I had nothing else to give or share at that time. When you are part of a collective and identify with the cumulative pain on physical, mental, emotional, and spiritual levels, it takes its toll. One time I was crying for someone who had died by suicide and my non-Indigenous friend asked why I was crying over someone I did not personally know. I replied that it is so sad and that I was feeling the collective grief. They agreed it must be very tough and added they never experienced such strong emotions for someone they did not know.

When I am experiencing collective grief or trauma, I remember I am connected to my place in my culture, my community, and the land I come from. There is strength for me to release the tears, the pain, and stay grounded in knowing "this too will pass." I come from a strong, resilient people and culture. My ancestors guide and support me. Others, too, are praying for one another in this time of deep sorrow and confusion. I can seek out the support I need.

Please feel free to draw or doodle anything that comes up for you. This is your memoir journal.

Journal Space: Have you ever experienced multiple grief and loss? Are you connected to any group you might identify with and have had to process how it has personally affected you? Take some time to honour yourself and your story and write what it means to you.

The article "The mental health of Aboriginal peoples: Transformation of identity and community" by Kirmayer et al. (2000)[10] addresses the social implications which occurred in the colonization of Canada and how this experience has affected Indigenous Peoples' mental health. Along with the establishment of the Indian residential school system, and the segregated pieces of land known as reserves and the creation of the Indian Act, colonial policies were enacted to control and govern Indigenous Peoples. These authors argue that it is imperative to consider how the contemporary legal and social oppression and marginalization of Indigenous culture and identity affects Indigenous mental well-being as it pertains to identity and self-esteem.

Specifically, the colonial oppressors outlawed Indigenous ceremonies and their ways of cultural being and when the children attended the Indian residential schools, they were punished for speaking their own languages. Taking these demoralizing experiences into consideration, one can make the argument that the research says that such negative experiences as this would have negative effects on Indigenous mental well-being. Oppressive practices imposed upon the Indigenous population were successful in eroding many of the people's connections to their land, language, culture, familial and community bonds, and thus caused erosion in their cultural pride, identity, and self-esteem.

I have memories which I believe connect identity to this discussion. For example, eating rabbit stew at my kookum's home and noticing how some Elders spoke our language to each other but not to the youth. I also recall how my father tried to pass stories on to me about the old ways and what he knew and understood about my Indigenous culture. He would share with me that his childhood was so much fun; he played freely with all the children in the community. They would spend hours hunting with their sling shots for squirrels and birds. Sometimes they would cook them up on a small fire they would make while out in the bush. No English was spoken in those early years when he was out on the land playing with his friends. These were good times and fun memories for him before he reached the age of five or six years old. Then the fun stopped when he started to attend school.

I believe those early childhood years helped form my dad's personality and some of his values. I recall feeling confused or disinterested in the stories my dad tried to tell me about the old ways because they were not at all what I was experiencing in my own childhood. I was uncomfortable trying to speak the language because I did not hear it spoken in my home or at school; everyone around me at this point spoke English often. The intergenerational effects and colonial influence—to not speak the language, to not talk about culture and ceremony—had taken hold in my early childhood.

Later when I attended university, I came across a book written by Hallowell (1992) about our community titled *The Ojibwa of Berens River, Manitoba Ethnography into History*.[11] This book put into words some of what my dad had been telling me. Afterward, I was able to talk with him and revisit the stories he had been trying to share with me. This time I was ready to listen and learn because I was now aware of what colonialism meant and what had occurred for us as Indigenous People. Being able to go through this process of rediscovery with my dad was very healing for me.

Journal Space: Do you have childhood or adolescent memories which connect you to your culture and family? Take some time to honour yourself and your story and write what it means to you.

Interpersonal Decolonization

The concept of decolonization is not a new term as it has its roots in the political and social sciences and Indigenous realms, but I first heard of it in academia. I have been learning about decolonization for the last several decades. I used the term decolonization to assist me with my personal healing, to help me change my ways of thinking, and to support my self-determination. I feel strong now and am grateful I have found answers that make sense for me.

Smith (2005) in Rowe et al. (2015) claims that "decolonization seeks to undo imperialism's subjugation and denigration of Indigenous Knowledges and culture" (p. 298).[12] The authors discussed decolonization for the purpose of challenging the structures of systemic power within academia and scholarly research and within many of the spaces that serve others in various professions, such as education, health, and the field component of social work practice. All professional designations that students graduate from within academia are based on knowledge from the Western worldview. The process of decolonization challenges colonialist settler mentalities and systemic oppressive systems to recognize and include other cultural ways of learning and understanding.

For my story and this journal, I explore the concept of decolonization and apply it within my story of healing and recovery. I explore decolonization and its application as an aspect of creating a new way to identify and strengthen my self-concept in my indigeneity. Through learning about decolonization and understanding how colonization continues to affect my mental health and well-being, I am now able to use the term decolonization as a path to deconstruct the lies and prejudices that were taught to me in my developmental years in childhood and adolescence. I learned about healing my inner child and that I can embrace my inner child and look back at those early developmental years and have empathy and self-compassion.

I took the initiative while learning about the history of colonization and its effects on Indigenous Peoples' mental health and well-being to apply it to my life. I began to use it as a process for my own healing and focused on healing my internalized oppression. I was now in a process of what I called interpersonal decolonization.

The personal process I have taken with decolonization is the path I have walked to accept, to love, and to understand myself more. I had to walk forward and process all those deep feelings of resentment, anger, shame, cultural self-hate, and confusion. Often, I would think too much about what others thought about me. It is that old issue of approval-seeking rearing its ugly head again. I had to let go of some of the Western worldview ways of defining my reality and how I understood myself. I had to embrace the cultural knowledge and understanding of who I was as it related to my Indigenous identity, thus deepening my sense of love and compassion for self and others. I am so grateful that I was able to overcome my cultural confusion and self-hate, eliminate my suicidal thoughts and feelings, and begin to truly heal. I now embrace my story and my journey toward self-determination, self-acceptance, and self-love.

As I think about what I have just written, I feel somewhat angry. Why do I feel this anger? Follow along with me here. Imagine you must learn to love and understand yourself by unlearning much of the reality you know. Imagine you learn about the history of colonization and how your ancestors and family were treated or are being treated. Think about learning why you do not speak your language and why you did not get to grow up going to powwows and other traditional ceremonies. Think about not knowing about healing medicines. All of these were outlawed and relegated to the underground or seen as blasphemy. This was the point where it became necessary for me to unlearn all I had been otherwise taught as in "decolonize myself" so I could proudly embrace my history, my culture, and my family story, and learn to love and accept who and what I was and where I came from. But it has been a real challenge because of how deeply I have been colonized.

When I feel anger, grief, and loss from the historical past that I know my ancestors and family have experienced, I have learned to let go of these emotions in healthy ways and affirm I am still here; we are still here, and we are strong and proud of who we are.

I become more balanced when I release the negative emotions. I can recognize the external colonial effects as the cause of them. I also remember I am worthy and complete, and my culture is strong, resilient, and has gifts that are within me that no person or system can erase. I can love myself and have self-compassion and compassion for others.

I have lived in urban areas since 1996 when I moved to Winnipeg, and I spent much of my time indoors as a child or in our store working when others were outside on the land, so I often feel disconnected from the traditional way of living on the land. To go camping and just be outside for long periods of time is foreign to me. However, I know that when I make the time to go and sit outside or take a drive to the beach or sit by a river, I can feel the healing energy of the land and I know I am connected.

My palate also changed due to disconnection from the land. The context of colonization, modernization, and living in urban areas removed me from eating many of the traditional foods that would probably be much healthier for me to eat and sustain my physical and spiritual well-being. I became accustomed to eating many processed foods and unaccustomed to eating traditional local foods.

I am now remembering to eat many more of our cultural foods, such as smoked suckerfish, boiled whitefish, and moose meat. I have been willing to try some of our cultural foods—such as moose liver, boiled fish heads, fish roe, or beaver tail—that I am not used to eating. They are a delicacy to my relatives yet taste so foreign to me. I have had to learn or relearn how to cook and prepare some types of cultural foods, and some are too unfamiliar, and I cannot eat them. I have learned to accept this about myself and do the best I can with this aspect of my decolonization process.

What I find so interesting is that smoked sucker and dried moose meat were my favourite foods when I was a child, and I really enjoy eating them when I have the opportunity. I do need more lessons on how to make a good duck soup or a roasted goose because I have tried, and it was a disaster. I remember once when I was still living back home, a friend's mom gave me several ducks to cook and I kept trying to cook them in a soup and it just didn't turn out, and my soup tasted horrible. I decided to stop trying and accept there are some tasks I am not going to be good at and leave it at that. My relatives and ancestors still love me, even when I do not or cannot enjoy some of the cultural foods and recipes offered to me. I remain worthy and I remain Indigenous. I am whole, perfect, and complete.

Please feel free to draw or doodle anything that comes up for you. This is your memoir journal.

Journal Space: Can you relate to this reality? Have you incorporated ways to access traditional foods that nurture you and your spirit, or is this something you desire to do? Take some time to honour yourself and your story and write what it means to you.

_____

_____

_____

_____

_____

_____

_____

_____

_____

_____

_____

_____

_____

_____

_____

_____

_____

_____

_____

_____

_____

_____

_____

_____

_____

_____

_____

_____

Seeing and Being Between Two Worldviews

Another issue associated with Indigenous people experiencing oppression because of colonization is the behaviour of turning the oppression toward each other. I have had other Indigenous people try to oppress me by saying I am "too rez" or "not rez enough." In the past, I would feel compelled to have to start explaining to others in this situation how I belong and how and why I identify myself as Indigenous. Now, I stay grounded as much as possible and recognize this is their perspective and opinion and they are entitled to it. I understand that it is part of colonization; those who have been oppressed begin to oppress one another.

At the same time, I do not have to take it on and allow it to alter my own sense of well-being. It is all related back to how we have all been colonized and I know I am doing my best to continually make sense of this reality I live in. I work toward having that self-acceptance and love and compassion for myself and others, but I know I am not perfect.

Renee Linklater, in her book *Decolonizing Trauma Work: Indigenous Stories and Strategies (2014),* discusses the differences between Indigenous and Western worldviews in how mental health and mental well-being are conceptualized and defined. Indigenous worldviews are wholistic and include the physical, mental, emotional, and spiritual aspects of oneself. They are inclusive of the relationship and connectedness to all things animate and inanimate, to the self and to the family and community,[13] whereas the Western worldview deals with the mind and behaviour separately, promoting mental health and well-being as an individualized issue that focuses on one's mind-cognition and body-physiology.

Understanding these differences is important and relevant for contributing to the decolonization process I have been going through. Likewise, the application of these differences is important for me to understand when I am working with other Indigenous people or emotionally supporting relatives and friends who have experienced the effects of this historical trauma. As Linklater explains, the concept of healing is different; the Indigenous healing path focuses on attaining balance within self and others, balance in the connectedness both internally and externally to all things and beings one is connected to.

Linklater also argues that Western labels for mental health diagnoses can be oppressive to those from Indigenous cultures because they are created from the Western worldview in their conceptualization and language and do not include Indigenous conceptualization, languages, and realities.

Therefore, Linklater recommends using the design of an Indigenous framework when supporting and assessing those who identify as Indigenous and are seeking services and treatment for challenges with their mental well-being. I personally had this experience when I sought help from a professional. Even though I did not fully understand the ideas and concepts in the framework, it helped me to realize how colonization and Western thought had totally overtaken my thinking and ways of being. I was able to learn more about myself and about how my Indigenous history and culture were part of who I am and that I was free to engage in a deeper level of self-awareness and growth, a deeper sense of healing my own self.

It is necessary to acknowledge the resilience of Indigenous people and how—despite the historical trauma from the past and current stressors of contemporary issues of prejudice, racism, and colonialism—many Indigenous people lead healthy and productive lives. Many have overcome these challenges and continue forward helping others on an ongoing basis and are fully self-determined.

Linklater suggests a respectful and appropriate way to provide support in mental health services is for practitioners to comprehend the historical oppressive experience as a form of trauma and to not minimize this by blaming the Indigenous person, family, or community for internalizing this historical trauma. Instead, Linklater recommends focusing on Indigenous Peoples' "resiliency" (p. 26) and to listen to how they have survived such atrocities and support their needs and desires to move forward. Indigenous people, families, and communities have what is described as "protective factors" (p. 26), such as "family networks, generational relationships, community support systems, cultural and spiritual resources and a shared collective history that bonds people together to create a sense of belonging" (p. 26).

When one comprehends it is the historical trauma and oppressive experiences that have greatly impacted Indigenous mental well-being, it is also necessary to be mindful and consider the reality that not every Indigenous person has dealt with issues pertaining to their mental health and well-being. The reality is that every Indigenous person has been affected by colonization whether they are aware of this or not, although they may not be experiencing any negative effects to their mental well-being. Everyone has been colonized. Some Indigenous people have assimilated deeply into the colonial landscape of Canada and thus know or understand little about their Indigenous ancestry and Indigenous ways of knowing and healing. Some Indigenous people and communities for whatever reason choose to remain involved in the various religions. We are all colonized in varying degrees, and this must also be respected. What is important is there is a choice and freedom to choose one's religious practice and spirituality as compared to when the cultural healing ways and ceremonies were outlawed. The ongoing struggle to change systemic racism and oppression remains.

On a personal level, Linklater's findings were affirming to me. I learned to stop blaming myself for my low moods and the negative issues I associated with my cultural identity as I understood how systemic oppressive policies and practices had contributed to how I had been feeling about myself. I was able to continue to participate in the cultural supports and healing spaces I knew were there and welcoming me to engage with. I continued to be involved with people and ceremony that enhanced my sense of well-being and connected me to my Indigeneity and my own spirit.

I continued my participation in several of the Indigenous ceremonies I had access to, such as the Sweat Lodge Ceremony, powwows, Sharing Circles, and the Smudge Ceremony which Linklater spoke of. I learned that my ancestors love and support me on my journey. They are always with me and are also part of my DNA, and my spirit has their genetic memory flowing through me. I am sent the support and guidance I need. I am provided a ceremony to witness and be in when I need this help or further understanding of what it means for me to be Indigenous and to keep healing the years of colonization that have affected and shaped me. This change of perspective from connecting to Linklaters's findings provided me with a deeper understanding of colonialism and its effects on my self-perception and attitudes.

Please feel free to draw or doodle anything that comes up for you. This is your memoir journal.

Journal Space: Can you relate to this historical reality, and have you been decolonizing yourself? Do you use the term decolonization in any circumstances in your life? Take time to honour yourself and your story and write what it means to you.

This is how it is, at least it is for me. I have been able to move through this decolonization process as best I could and now, I fully embrace who I am. I accept and love all of me—even the angry part of myself. I remember a time when I was with my Elder who helped and supported me so much. She told me to let myself feel my anger, for in not doing so I would be out of balance. She told me I was "too nice," and this was not being in balance. She gave me this teaching and so I learned to allow the anger and loss I was feeling and was able to move through it to a place of balance. I learned to process it without continuing to blame myself as bad, wrong, or unworthy, without taking a drink of alcohol or a mind-altering substance, and to just feel the feeling and process it as best I could. This teaching was so empowering. It has been an emotionally challenging and transformative journey. I am an Indigenous, Ojibway, mixed-blood, cisgender, heterosexual woman who has been colonized and lives assimilated in the Canadian context. I have self-compassion for who I am and how I present myself in the world.

I know of many others who have been on this journey, others who have chosen to go down the path of the traditional lifestyle—healing themselves, for example, in powwow dance or Sundance ceremony— while still others have chosen differently. I chose to move forward as an observer in the powwow and the Sundance ceremony healing ways but did not specifically take up becoming a powwow dancer or commit to the requirements necessary to participate in the Sundance ceremony. I respect myself, my choices, and my right to self-determination. However, I also have the utmost respect for those I know who live the traditional way of life.

The freedom is in the reality that I now have a choice of how I want to live my life and how I choose to live my spirituality. My ancestors and parents did not have choices. As I see some of my relatives and friends demonstrate their beliefs in Christianity, they share they are now Christian by choice and not by force. Here again, I also respect their choices and their journey.

Once when I was in Montreal for a work trip, I went for a walk by myself and found the Notre-Dame Basilica. I stood outside for a few minutes, looking up at the tall steeple and the big doors in front of me. Many people were walking up the stairs around me. I took a deep breath and then I walked up the stairs and went inside. I could hear the organ music playing and could see different people making their genuflections and signs of the cross with the holy water and then kneeling. I could smell the incense burning. Others were in another area making offerings and lighting candles. I wondered what everyone was praying for or going through. I found a bench and sat.

The memories began to flood in, taking me back to being in church in my childhood and the catechism lessons I attended. I remembered the rituals of the genuflections and signs of the cross that I had been taught as a child, and I easily did them before I kneeled and said my prayer, and then sat back up on the bench, feeling its hard, cool surface beneath me. Tears started to fall from my eyes. I sat there and wept for my inner child and my inner adolescent self. I sat there, and I just let my tears fall. I cried for all the painful memories I had and all the confusion. As I sat there, I made peace with my kookum and myself, and I made peace with my parents. This was a big part of my forgiveness process on that day. I walked out of the basilica feeling so free and cleansed from the tears I shed and releasing myself from the old painful stories I had been hanging on to.

Some of these old hurts and painful feelings resurfaced with the recent recovery of the unmarked graves of the children buried at the Indian residential schools. I felt compassion for myself, our mother, and our grandmother— my kookum had been at the Cowessess Indian residential school for many years.

I believed the stories when I heard former Survivors sharing their truths. I was more shocked and horrified that Canadians were surprised by this reality when I heard some people share that they had never heard about Indian residential schools.

I have friends and relatives who walk in many different spiritual and healing spaces. I can find someone to speak with, I can make an offering of tobacco to seek council from an Elder, I can go to a ceremony and witness another's healing, I can sit in nature and lean against a tree and speak with my Creator, or I can ask my Christian relatives and friends to pray for me. I have wonderful cultural relationships and options to connect with.

North – I Am Home

I name the direction of the North in this section because I have now surpassed my sixtieth year of travelling around the sun. The north in my Medicine Wheel is about being older and comfortable with myself and others. I am in a place of accepting how things have unfolded in my life, and I have insight to who I am and what I believe, think, and feel. In this place of acceptance, I very much connect to the reality of knowing that I may not have made all the correct decisions along the way but that I made the best ones I could in each part of my journey so far. Although colonialism can still affect me personally, I know I have options and spiritual help to support myself on navigating those effects.

The historical effects of colonialism discussed within the literature and through my personal experience created my cultural confusion, shame, and thus my internalized oppression. As a result, I struggled with that sense of belonging. Beginning early in my life, I struggled to define myself and who I was. As a child, I felt as though I didn't fit in anywhere and that there was something wrong with me. In my early adolescence, I began disassociating from anything or anyone Indigenous and denying my cultural identity.

Further into my adolescence when I was sixteen years old, I learned about the Métis and the connection my mother and grandparents had to this identity. I started to realize and understand I was Indigenous but did not know anything about what this truly meant. When I later began learning about colonialism, the Canadian government's assimilation policies, the relationships between the churches and state, and that Indigenous Peoples were given labels and numbers through the Indian Act, it felt like I had been broken open. I needed to embrace my cultural understanding and finally decided to claim my Indigenous identity at the age of twenty-nine through Bill C-31 and receive First Nations Status under the Indian Act.

I have gratitude for our community and to those political leaders and social activists who created this transformational change in Canada for Indigenous Peoples and specifically disenfranchised Indigenous women. When someone I knew was struggling with their own internalized oppression and suggested we go back to identifying as Métis, I said, "No way. After all the years of therapy to overcome this cultural confusion, I'm staying on the path I am on. I will continue to identify as First Nations." This has been my process of cultural reclamation.

This journey of cultural reclamation and understanding how colonialism has affected me is not unique to me. I think it is continually occurring at various levels within individuals, families, communities, and nations. It is an ongoing complex journey. I think of the article by Ermine titled "The Ethical Space of Engagement" (2007). Ermine denotes that Canadians and Indigenous Peoples all function in spaces which are constructed and governed by laws and values of the Western worldview. Ermine proposes there is a space between the Western and Indigenous worlds and peoples where an ethics of engagement can be created for the equality of sharing to occur. He proposes that in this ethical space, the sharing will be reciprocal with a commitment to set aside differences and a commitment to hear one another and listen to what the other is saying.[14]

For example, I have often witnessed that when a non-Indigenous person is listening to an Indigenous person sharing their experience with racism or about how they live and understand their cultural reality, the non-Indigenous listener may feel uncomfortable and think it necessary to give their own example of how they went through similar experiences. I've been told by the non-Indigenous person they feel a need to try to identify with the Indigenous speaker and to connect in some manner. I know I have had to learn the skill of listening to another when they are sharing their personal perspectives. I aim to listen with intent, to witness, to be present, and to not make the dialogue and interaction about me.

An important part of learning is to listen with empathy, be open to understanding, and be mindful of the context that this sharing is occurring within. I encourage listeners to give an individual the space to

When I feel overwhelmed and unheard as I am sharing how I experience my cultural oppression, I can reaffirm that my voice and story are valid through my own self-determination. Alternatively, I can find someone I trust to vent with and share how I am feeling so I can process the experience and let it go. There are loving spaces and people who willingly listen and support me. I know my ancestors are also doing this for me.

share how they are experiencing their reality and how they self-identify as an Indigenous person. The listener needs to be aware and intuitive or ask specifically what the speaker may want in this communication. Often, Indigenous Peoples want the validation that we are different and to be respected for this difference. The point is to acknowledge there are differences in how one experiences the world, and the history of colonialism has been detrimental to Indigenous Peoples.

Please feel free to draw or doodle anything that comes up for you. This is your memoir journal.

Journal Space: Do you have a place and space to share openly with others? Take some time to honour yourself and your story and write what it means to you.

_____

_____

_____

_____

_____

_____

_____

_____

_____

_____

_____

_____

_____

_____

_____

_____

_____

_____

_____

_____

_____

_____

_____

_____

_____

_____

_____

_____

_____

_____

_____

_____

_____

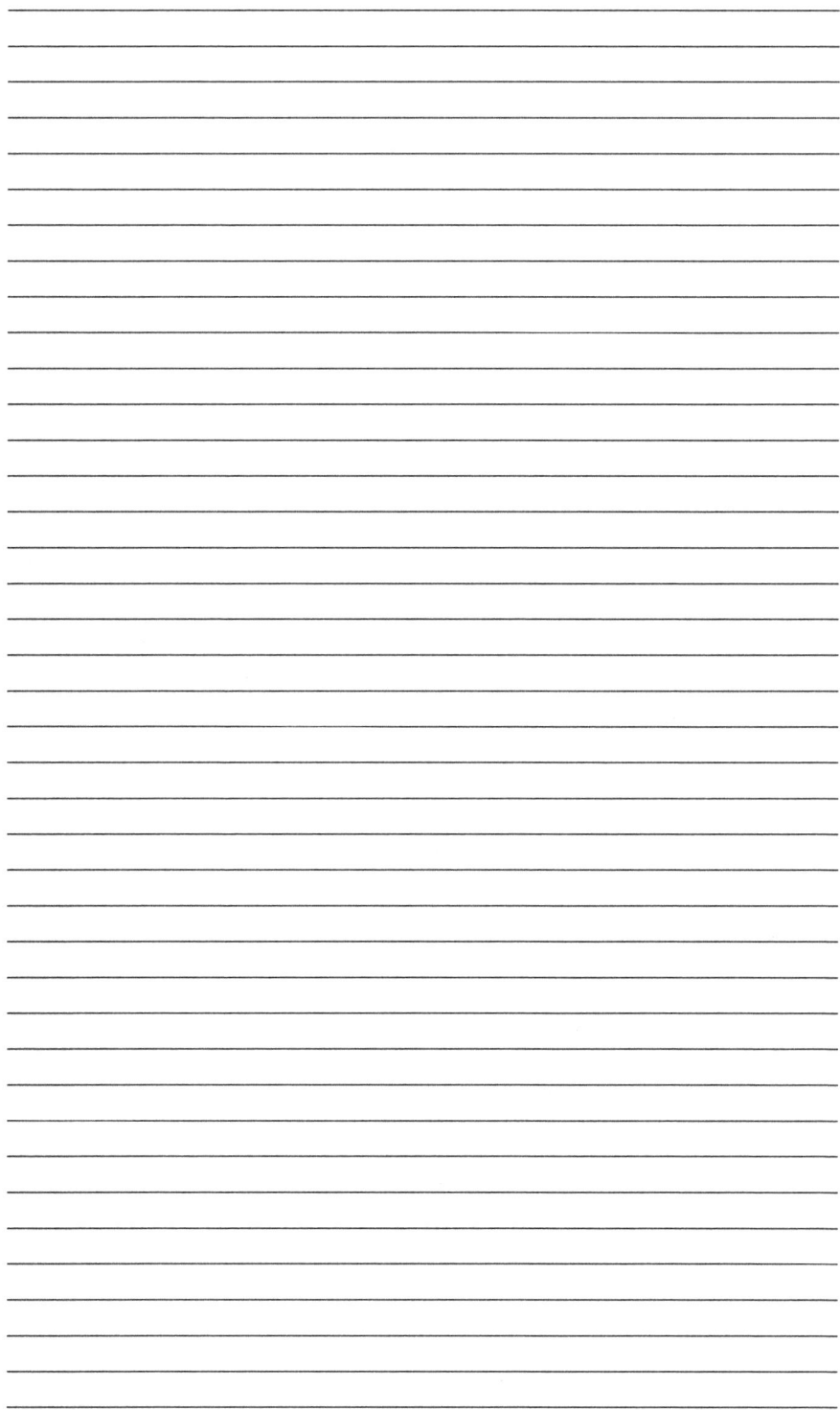

Connections to Ceremony, Community, and Traditional Cultural Practices

I started understanding more about myself and my Indigenous cultural identity from what I learned from the research and by making the decision to participate in some of the traditional Indigenous ceremonies. I learned to embrace the opportunities that I felt would help me heal and I began to connect to the different ceremonies, community gatherings, and traditional cultural practices. I have taken this action as part of my Medicine Wheel to come into further balance and self-determination.

I have attended many Sharing Circles where the Smudge Ceremony was used, and I was able to release my feelings and thoughts and share in the sacred space what I needed to say. There were also instances when I sat in the Sharing Circle and just let my tears flow for others sharing their stories, and I did not have to speak. I was able to witness and connect with them through similarities in our experiences. Listening to another speak can provide powerful results. For example, I remember a time when I was being disrespectful and—I can honestly say—"mean" to my mom. My mom and I were in a Sharing Circle and in this ceremony, she spoke up for herself and literally told me she was not going to accept any more blame from me about our family. She said she had made her amends and from that day forward she would not take any further disrespect. I heard my mom clearly and I owned my poor behaviour. In that moment, I silently released all the stories and resentful feelings I had been carrying that were negatively affecting me and my relationship with her. I decided in that moment to behave differently and opened myself up to loving and healing our relationship. I focused on forgiveness and love for myself and for her. This was an enormously transformative circle we sat in that day.

I also received my spiritual name in the Sweat Lodge ceremony. Through receiving my traditional spiritual name and using it when in ceremony, I was taught that my ancestors and spiritual guides would recognize me when I prayed and participated. It felt so positive to me to be seen, heard, and recognized as equal during the Sharing Circle. The Elders and helpers in these healing spaces took care of me and my emotional needs. These experiences helped to heal me and gave me courage and strength.

Likewise, when friends invited me to attend a Sundance ceremony, I accepted this invitation and went with my husband. It was such a beautiful sacred experience, and I accepted all the love and the healing that was taking place. We sat in the kitchen area where helpers were lovingly preparing food for everyone to eat. There was laughter and joy and stories being shared with one another. My friend gently reminded me of various Protocols we needed to be mindful of and respect while we were there. I wore my long ceremonial skirt that my mother had made me, and I felt good about being reminded about what was expected of me while attending this ceremony.

My friend encouraged us to sit near the arbour where the dancing was occurring. The sun was shining and there was a gentle breeze blowing. My husband rested in his chair beside me and nodded off into what appeared a peaceful sleep.

The dancers were both male and female adults, and they were within an arbour made of poplar trees that were still planted in the earth; the arbour was an enclosed circle with one opening. I could not see directly because the branches and leaves of the trees blocked my view, allowing privacy and respecting the sacredness of the healing space the dancers were in. I had glimpses of the participants with their backs to me and I could see they were shaking their trees and I could hear the Eagle whistle blowing. The Eagle whistle gave them strength as they danced for the duration of the drums and songs being sang.

My friend quietly explained to me that these dancers each had a tree to stand with and they would dance and shake their tree while the singers were singing and beating the drums. The dancing and tree-shaking would go on for as long as the drums and singing went on. These dancers did this without any water or food for four days and nights. They would only rest when the drums stopped and then sit by their tree until the drums beat again. Those of us who were there as witnesses and supporters were directed to not take any food or water to the dance area out of respect for the participants who were dancing.

I prayed for everyone who was dancing and for everyone who was there during this time. I could hear the drums beating and the scent of the medicines burning. I closed my eyes and basked in this healing moment. I recognized many faces, but I did not say anything to anyone while near the ceremony. I wanted to respect this was a healing sacred space, but within my heart I felt a part of this group. The people I knew were also connected to people I loved and respected; this gave me a real feeling of interconnectedness. I did not need to be recognized or acknowledged or for them to know who I was. I was there to witness and support and was gifted my own healing thoughts and feelings. This was such a blessing. I used this experience to give me strength to keep working on this book and to stay on the path of loving and living my life. I left the ceremony with my heart filled with gratitude for the strength of the ceremonies and the teachings, for the healing those who were dancing were giving and receiving, and so grateful I could be a witness in this sacred space.

I once attended a large ceremony called The Wiping Away the Tears which comes from the Lakota People. This was for people who had experienced a loss, and the ceremony dealt with grief. I know some of our families have multiple losses beginning in childhood up to their adulthood. I sat as an observer in this ceremony. It was healing to sit and witness the participants as they addressed their many losses and released the grief they had been carrying. Prayers and Protocols were being conducted, drummers were drumming, rattles were shaking, and deep sharing occurred with the scent of the smudge cleansing the area throughout the ceremony. Supported by the Elders and helpers in the circle, participants were wrapped in star blankets made for them especially for this healing ceremony. I remember sitting in the outer circle and letting my own tears flow to release the grief of what I had been holding in my body and spirit at that time. I walked away from this ceremony in awe of the power that ceremonial healing can bring to those who participate.

When my spirit feels worn out from the work to decolonize myself, and the layers of systemic oppression feel heavy on my heart as a collective pain, I restore myself and my spirit through attending ceremonial gatherings, walking in the woods, sitting by a river, or talking to a trusted friend. My spirit guides me to what I need to do, where I need to be, and to spend time with whom I want.

Please feel free to draw or doodle anything that comes up for you. This is your memoir journal.

Journal Space: Do you go to ceremony or have the desire to reclaim a part of your culture? What rituals and ceremony do you participate in to support your well-being? Take time to honour yourself and your story and write what it means to you.

The strength of community support can be far-reaching and intergenerational in a positive way as well. I remember a time I was in our family store tending the cash register when I was eleven or twelve years old. On this day, one of our Elders had died and I was feeling sad and had a few tears running down my cheek. Another older customer asked me what was wrong, and I shared with him that I was sad this person had died. The Elder who had passed was in his eighties or maybe even older. The man that I was talking to put his hand on my shoulder and said, "You know, omakakii"—he called me by the nickname given to me by some of the Elders sitting outside our store at the time of my birth—"do not cry for long. It was kind of you to feel sad and honour this Elder. But in our ways, you must know he lived a good long life and we all will have our time to leave this life. Be happy for him that he did live long and was loved by so many. Remember him in a good way, and this will help you with your loss and sad feelings. We go to the spirit world, but our spirit lives on, and you can always just talk to him when you miss or remember him, and he will know you are there." Afterward, I felt much better, and I never forgot the teaching this kind man in our community gave to me.

Diagnosis and Healing in the Indigenous Context

The article, "Diagnosis as a naming ceremony: Caution warranted in use of the DSM-IV with Canadian Aboriginal peoples," by Overmars (2010) discusses how the *Diagnostic and Statistical Manual of Mental Disorders, Fourth Edition* (DSM-IV) is often used to diagnose Aboriginal people with mental disorders, and this practice by mental health professionals has its limitations because the diagnosis may not take into consideration the context and cultural worldviews of the Aboriginal person.[15] Much like Linklater (2014), Overmars argues for the need to be mindful that the diagnoses and labels within the DSM-IV are based on Western cultural worldviews and do not consider Indigenous ways of knowing. These Western diagnoses and labels have been validated through scientific positivistic research based on the myth that there is only "one truth" (Overmars, 2010, p. 81). In the Indigenous worldviews, there are many truths from multiple sources which include traditional teachings, empirical observations, and revelations. The label of post-traumatic stress disorder (PTSD) is in the DSM-IV, and Overmars proposes there are limitations to this research because smaller portions of the population are excluded in the research relevant to the label and diagnosis of PTSD.

What is not included in the DSM-IV in the post-traumatic stress disorder category is historical trauma. Historical trauma is different from PTSD because it includes intergenerational trauma—multiple traumas can be experienced within the family and be passed onto other generations. Evans-Campbell in Overmars (2010) argues this does a "disservice not only to Aboriginal peoples but to other cultural groups which suffer from intergenerational trauma, such as holocaust survivors and newcomers from war zones" (p. 81). This is valuable contextual and experiential information that is relevant and different from PTSD and has different effects to one's mental health and well-being.

Overmars main thesis in this article is for mental health practitioners to be mindful of how and why the DSM-IV is being used and to be cognizant when using this information that it does not consider Indigenous cultural worldviews. Indigenous Peoples' historical and cultural experience are marginalized by this exclusion yet again. I make the argument here for mental health service providers to consider how the individual being assessed be seen and understood from their own Indigenous worldview and positionality. Moreover, it is necessary for mental health service providers to seek knowledge and understanding of the historical and current context of Indigenous Peoples wherever they locate themselves when providing supportive mental health services. This would be a culturally respectful and trauma-informed way of practicing.

It is more beneficial to me if a practitioner (or any person) hears my story—and my beliefs and how I see and experience the world—with an open mind and heart before they make any judgements or recommendations. Context plays a significant factor in how someone presents themselves in their relationships from an interpersonal and intrapersonal perspective. I was often questioned about my Indigenous identity by people from other cultures and even people from my own culture and this would often upset me and cause me to doubt myself. I was expected to explain how I identify as Indigenous.

I would often be corrected by people or challenged as to what gave me the knowledge to say this. For example, they may question me to explain in further detail why I don't dance powwow or why I don't know in detail the teachings of a path of spirituality from an Indigenous perspective, and it feels like an interrogation. Sometimes I was judged negatively for not being an expert on my Indigenous culture and not being a fluent language speaker. I felt so angry and frustrated and hurt when this would happen. It is unethical and unprofessional to ask anyone from another culture for justification about how and why they locate themselves within their culture and say to them, for example, "tell me how and why you identify as Irish, French, White, Jewish or African."

There were also instances where I experienced oppression and exclusion by others who identify as Indigenous but did not see me as Indigenous or Indigenous enough. I would be questioned as to why I am a certain way or why I am not doing everything in my power to learn to become fluent in the language. How it affects me depends on who is asking and how they are asking when they inquire about my Indigenous identity. It might launch me into memories of being or feeling oppressed. At such times I feel a range of feelings, like anger, self-doubt, anxiety, and unworthiness.

Once when I was teaching, I had a student share with me that it was the first time in four years of being in university he ever felt so comfortable, included, heard, and supported to share his voice and stories from his culture and how he saw and experienced the world. This student was validating my ability to create a space, inclusive of this student's stories and experiences. This made me feel good because of all the learning and growing I had accomplished. I had achieved a goal for myself when I received this feedback from this student. It was my intention to be a teacher who could create a space where my students would feel seen, heard, and included.

In another situation I was witness to an Indigenous student who would not listen to the instructions and advice that an Indigenous instructor was providing on how to complete an assignment. That student went to a non-Indigenous faculty member for the same advice. The Indigenous instructor clearly understood it was an example of how Indigenous Peoples can come to oppress one another. The Indigenous student could not trust in the Indigenous instructor but could trust a non-Indigenous one.

> When I feel oppressed by someone from my own culture, and they cannot see this behaviour in themselves, I remind myself I am worthy and competent; I have compassion for myself and others in how colonization has affected us.

I had an interest in psychology while I was in university. I learned about various labels people are diagnosed with when they have issues in their lives that affect their mental health. One day while working with my supervisor in the psychology department as a school psychology associate, I shared my thoughts about mental health diagnoses and labels with him because I had been experiencing a lot of anxiety and worrisome thoughts. I knew I had issues with my self-esteem while I did my best to work in this department as the school psychology associate. I also knew the feelings I was experiencing were connected to my cultural identity—I almost felt like a traitor to my culture for trying to be a school psychologist. I explained to my supervisor that several years earlier I had gone to a physician and was given the diagnosis and label of Generalized Anxiety Disorder (GAD). I had become a worrier, worrying about many people and situations most of the time throughout my day.

Everything I learned about psychology had been based on the Western worldview. I told my supervisor, "I think if I were going to give myself a mental health diagnosis or label, I would suggest it be Internalized Oppression Anxiety Disorder." It was a more appropriate label for what I was experiencing. This has been part of my journey to overcome the effects of everything I have been sharing, find a way to decrease worry and anxiety, and increase my overall sense of peace and well-being. To this end, I still like my label better.

When my internalized oppression becomes activated, I remind myself to be still and know I am enough. My Medicine Wheel of life is my journey. My spirit is strong, my ancestors love and hold me safe in their strength. I can use my ceremonial name or a name my family has given me to ground myself and know I am heard, seen, and recognized.

Journal Space: Can you relate to this history and reality? What labels are you defining yourself by and does your Indigenous history and identity connect to them? Take some time to honour yourself and your story and write what it means to you.

Facilitating the women's group when I was completing my Master of Social Work advanced field placement validated the need for sacred healing spaces within a cultural context. Many Indigenous Peoples have experienced different forms of abuse, and some want these culturally appropriate spaces to process what is heavy in their heart and spirit. I know that I am comfortable on most days to embrace different ways of healing between the Indigenous worldview and the Western worldview, but there is truly a difference. I think more than ever now there is an increase in desire to connect with one another as Indigenous Peoples. Some Indigenous people prefer to only use the teachings and ceremonies of their cultures, and some choose a combination of the two worlds. I have chosen to walk my path and accept I can participate in both.

> I am free to choose how I live, see, and experience the world. My ancestors fought and died for this freedom; my culture supports my journey and the freedom of my own volition. For example, I can choose to eat moose meat, or I can eat pizza; I can pray with tobacco, or I can choose to pray to Jesus. The point is I am Indigenous. My ancestors gave their lives for my freedom of choice, and I am grateful.

Healing Deeper Means Loving and Accepting Myself

I believe that I was sexually abused as a child, but I do not remember who my abuser was or when, what, and where it happened. What I do know is that I had a major physical and emotional reaction one time where I was in an appointment for a health check-up. After this appointment was completed, I left the building and I felt horrible, I was shaking, and I wanted to just cry, and I felt like I was a little girl approximately four or five years old. The health practitioner had not been inappropriate, but the experience activated something inside of me; it set off this visceral reaction. I called a trusted friend to talk to and I asked her if she would come and sit with and support me while I shared in confidence what I had experienced.

I could not remember who the perpetrator was, and I let go of trying to figure it out and chose to heal by accessing counselling and ceremony. I learned it was not my fault and I focused on loving myself and strengthening my own well-being. Attending the Sweat Lodge ceremonies and Sharing Circles were a big part of stabilizing my well-being. I sought therapy for these memories and learned to use the cognitive behaviour techniques—such as grounding or the five senses—in the moment to help regulate my moods when triggers or memories happen. I also saw a therapist who specialized in a type of therapy called Eye Movement Desensitization and Reprocessing (EMDR). This was a powerful and helpful therapeutic way to deal with trauma. I processed past issues and traumatic experiences. I learned to create a safe space in my mind and spirit to envision transferring those thoughts and emotions into this container of my own design. I found people and spaces—such as ceremony—that I felt safe with to heal this part of my past.

The healing work I completed helped me to learn to love and tenderly care for my inner child and to be able to remain in my adult self. I know the past is over, and I still can have memories or situations that reactivate how I felt as a young child, adolescent, or adult. By learning how to tend to myself when I am in that emotional state, I have grown calmer and more peaceful.

> It may be that there is intergenerational pain and linkages to the past that I need to deal with and be open to healing. My ancestors and spiritual guides love and support me, and my familial roots are strong. When I choose to heal myself and love myself more deeply, I become more loving outwardly and give compassion to myself and others.

My Spiritual Bundle

A spiritual bundle consists of items that are deemed sacred to the individual who puts them together for the purpose of participation in practicing their form of spirituality. This could be in various ceremonies or in personal prayer with self and others. The bundle may consist of traditional Indigenous items, such as a smudge bowl, an eagle feather or feathers, rattles, and medicines such as sweet grass, sage, tobacco, or cedar, different types and colours of cloth, a talking stick, or rocks called grandfathers and grandmothers. I have such a bundle, but I also use this title *My Spiritual Bundle* to include what I participated in to help me heal. I will still attend counselling sessions, twelve-step groups, sit in prayer and meditation with my smudge bowl, and attend ceremonies such as the Sharing Circle and Sweat Lodge when I think it is necessary to do so.

Counselling

I first found support from individual counsellors who were non-Indigenous and, I suspect, probably did not even understand much of my cultural context and confusion. But they did offer me a space to work on issues that were troubling me most at the time, and these sessions assisted in increasing my own level of self-awareness. Attending the counselling sessions provided me the emotional support and encouragement to continue focusing on learning new ways of thinking and being that I felt I needed.

> The one behaviour I am grateful for is learning to reach out for help when I was feeling lost or alone.

Twelve-step groups

I visited several twelve-step groups, and I experienced a sense of belonging when I went and spent time at them. I eventually became a regular member of a group, and I enjoyed recovering in a group process; it helped me to not feel so alone. I secured a new relationship with a person who was a stranger to me, but I liked the message she was carrying, and I asked her to be my guide and mentor. It was through the group process of this self-help program that I really healed much of what was troubling me. I am forever grateful to the women who have guided me in my years of healing and recovery. They have been part of my life and recovery program and supported my journey, helping me in so many ways with my self-development to become the woman I wanted to be. Simultaneously, I was gathering more knowledge and understanding of my culture, and I was reclaiming and growing this part of myself. This supported my self-determination.

> Healing alone from issues of addiction, abuse, and trauma can take its toll on a person. It is okay to seek support and guidance from trusted counsellors, healers, or a dear friend who you know can handle what you need to share as they are able to be your sacred witness. If I am scared to look within by myself, my Creator is with me, and I will know who it is safe to share my story with. I heal and grow stronger when I bring my challenges to the light, when I talk with someone that I feel is safe to talk with, and when I attend ceremony or another type of spiritual/religious gathering.

I also found the book, *The Red Road to Wellbriety in the*

Native American Way (2002).[16] This book was and is a great support for my well-being. It makes me feel so good because it speaks to commonalities between the recovery programs I participate in and Native American ways of living. Within the book, as well as within twelve-step literature, it is recommended that one find a God or a higher consciousness of their own understanding outside of oneself. This was an aspect of the recovery process that I fully engaged in and connected with.

Smudge bowl and prayer

I have learned that in our Indigenous cultural belief systems, everything has a life and spirit, be they animate or inanimate. A large part of my spirituality is my practice of using my smudge bowl. This bowl I use is a source of strength and is a holding space for all my feelings, my gratitude, and my prayers, including prayers for others or prayers that may be requested. It is half of an abalone shell, with sequined colours of varying shades of gray, white, turquoise, and silver. My bowl has burned many offerings of the medicines of tobacco, sage, cedar, and sweet grass depending on what has been occurring for me when I light a smudge. It serves me so well and it is full of love for me and my well-being. I often use the visualization of my smudge bowl when I have had troublesome thoughts or feelings and I

My spiritual smudge bowl

am unable to do a physical smudge. I imagine transferring all those thoughts and feelings to my bowl to hold them there until I can light a smudge and cleanse them from my being. This has been an immensely helpful practice I have learned to do in the moment to support myself.

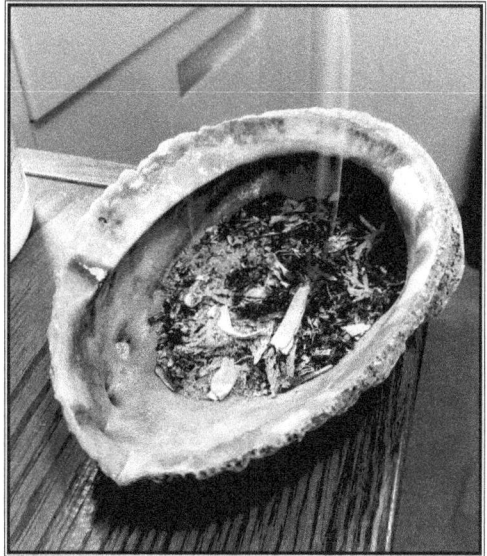

Circle or ceremony

There are days when it feels like I have no time for my personal needs. The beauty in the struggle is being able to connect to places and spaces with people I identify with culturally. So, I go to a circle or a ceremony, and it does not matter what part I play in this space; I am there for a reason and know I belong. I can receive the healing energy and emotional release from being there, whether as a witness or a participant.

Higher power

I believe in a power greater than myself, and I choose to call this power Creator, God, or Creator God. I am also learning about my higher consciousness. I am not attached to any of these labels for my spiritual understanding, but what I am attached to is the understanding and belief that there is a spirit or energy that is outside of me that gives me strength, and I have faith in it. I know that I am not alone, and the outcomes in the grand scheme of things are not solely of my own making. I do what I can as a human being and let go of the outcome. I know the little girl inside me is happier when I am loving myself and believing in myself, because this is what she needed and wanted when she was a young child.

> I am aware of my race, culture, gifts, and privileges, and I gratefully acknowledge them and use them to support and make space for others. I am interested in learning from others.

Nature, exercise, and playfulness

Likewise, the little girl inside me can go hug a tree, sit outside on the grass, and watch any nature that surrounds us. I can breathe and know my strength comes from my ancestors and from the land.

Physical exercise supports my well-being. I like to golf regularly in the summer months as this sport brings me such joy. I love being outside, breathing in the smell of the land and grass on the course, and the friendships I have made with other golfers. Another summer activity I enjoy is riding my bike. I also have an old exercise bike which I ride indoors when the weather turns.

I colour and do paint-by-number kits and am learning more about free painting. I let my five-year-old inner child out to enjoy the fun I feel doing these types of activities. It is very relaxing, and I feel playful when doing them.

I have also participated in various small beading projects. A beading workshop to honour Missing and Murdered Indigenous Women & Girls was a significant cultural and healing event. These activities connect me to memories of my childhood when I would watch my great auntie do her beading. I especially enjoy doing these projects in a group setting.

Journaling

I journal regularly in the mornings upon my awakening. I write out my thoughts and feelings about what is on my mind and in my heart as I connect with the physical, mental, emotional, and spiritual parts of myself. I also write about any of my sleep time dreams, possible goals I might want to achieve, and I end each session with at least three to five entries of what I am grateful for. My journaling continues to support my mental well-being.

Implicit Cultural Values

I have some memories from childhood that provided me with the teachings of my community and my culture. There has always been nurturing and love associated with the gathering of friends and family and the sharing of food. The giving and sharing of what one has with one another is an Indigenous cultural value—the value of generosity, which is a strong value of our people.

I learned to always make a little extra when I cooked meals because we never knew if someone might drop by. This way, we were ready and prepared to share a meal with them. I learned this value of generosity by watching how my kookum treated visitors and other relatives when they dropped in at her home when I was there visiting. My grandparents would always offer their visitors whatever they were eating, or my kookum would prepare something for them to eat. They always made room around their table for everyone.

Through attending and participating in the Sharing Circles and the Sweat Lodge ceremony, I learned that eating is a spiritual process. Berries are brought into the Sweat Lodge to feed the spirits of the ancestors as well as the animal spirits and to feed the spirits of those in attendance. There is also a sharing of food after each ceremony is completed. I would observe someone at each ceremony also making a plate of food with items on it from the meal to put out for the ancestors and animal spirits. I connected to this spiritual process and at times I will put an extra plate at the table for any member of my family that has passed away to honour their spirit. In other instances, I may set an extra plate in case someone happens to drop by when we are sitting down to eat. This has become a personal, spiritual, and intuitive practice for me.

I remember a business trip to New Mexico. We went to eat at one of the traditional Navajo restaurants and on our table, there was a "spirit bowl." We were told we could put some of the food in the bowl while we ate and then they would make the spiritual offering for our relatives or spirit guides after the meal. The teachings of generosity, sharing, and caring is part of other Indigenous cultures as it is mine. I thought this was so awesome, and I now have a spirit bowl in my kitchen for the same purpose.

Other cultural teachings I received were to take only what I need, and to give thanks by putting tobacco down if something is taken from the land, or animals are to be eaten, or when sharing a big meal with family and friends. I remember once being with a spiritual Elder and I was complaining that I was starving. He asked me, "Have you ever really starved for food in your life?"

I thought about his question. "No," I replied.

"Then be grateful you are only hungry. Try not to say you are starving ever again when you are just hungry," he said.

Much of my learning and growth has been in moments such as this. I come from a culture that is non-directive and very moment centred. When it is the right time, the teacher and learning will transpire.

In my forties, I went through a naming ceremony to receive my spiritual traditional name. The Elder who conducted the ceremony and gave me my name told me that this name is for me because I can move through my emotions that sometimes can be extremely high and exceptionally low; it depends on what I am experiencing. He also said it was for me as a helper because I help many people with their emotions, and I work as a therapist and in mental health. I arranged for my son to go to a naming ceremony in his teens and he is free to connect with his name and the teachings as he chooses. I use mine when I pray or am in ceremonies; otherwise, I keep it private.

Please feel free to draw or doodle anything that comes up for you. This is your memoir journal.

Journal Space: Do you have memories or experiences where you have learned teachings applicable to your life? Take time to honour yourself and your story and write what it means to you.

Balance – I am HOME, I am my CULTURE

My life is like many others who have experienced emotional pain and loss. What is different for me, as I am now into my sixties, is the fact that I have stopped running from my painful life experiences. Instead, I choose to process my feelings and determine in each moment what is the next choice I must make or want to make. I remember that I am my culture and I think or pause and connect with my own spirit to understand where I may need to bring myself into balance within my Medicine Wheel.

I am reminded of the teachings I learned from *The Sacred Tree*, from different teachings from my Elder, and from many years sitting in meetings of twelve-step groups and ceremony. I have been living a life of sobriety for several decades, and I believe in the saying, "Wherever you go, there you are." There is nowhere for me to run because I take myself with me wherever I go. I have lived in several different towns and dwellings, and in each part of my life I have still had to take responsibility for my choices and my feelings in my experiences. The teachings I have received from my Indigenous Elders also remind me that "I am." It is important to be who I am and not have to put on any other masks, to just be accepting of who I am and how I show up in each moment on my path. I have learned to look within and reflect on where I am in my Medicine Wheel of my life, and to ask myself what I need to do or feel to find my way back or forward to balance.

Embracing myself in my Medicine Wheel—all aspects of my physical, mental emotional, and spiritual self—helps me to reconcile the differences between teachings I have learned from the Indigenous worldview and those parts of me that are affected and ingrained from being born into colonization. I have learned to focus on my self-determination, and I do the work to increase my own self-awareness and self-reflection. The connection I find within the different aspects of my Medicine Wheel leads me into my centre of balance and has led me to healing and to understanding my personal strengths and gifts.

146

Instead of running away from challenging circumstances and feelings when I know my emotions are all over the place, or "dysregulated," I choose to be still and stay exactly where I am and look inward. I am mindful I can do this because I do not live in any physical danger. When emotionally challenging times come upon me, I choose not to run anywhere or change anything. I choose to look inward and commit to loving myself and understanding what is occurring for me. I also use a cultural context to continue my healing from the intergenerational traumas brought on from the past. Once I have completed this process for myself, I then decide what is the next right thing for me to do. I have learned to respond and not react in most instances.

When I judge myself or believe I am wrong for my choices, or I think that others do not understand or approve of how I live my life, I am willing to walk through the emotional pain of the situation and give myself time and space to process what is occurring for me. I remember I have full control of my own life and the choices I make.

My family may be like many other Indigenous families. We have been affected by colonization; we face issues such as addictions to alcohol, substances, sex, and work, sexual abuse, family violence, and many layers of loss and separation. It is a heavy burden to carry when you come to know there are so many layers of intergenerational trauma within families and communities. At first, my trauma response was to either fight, flee, or freeze, but mostly I froze. Once I began to thaw out, I chose my methods of healing as I needed and wanted. This has been a time of deeper self-reflection and transformational change. I have deepened my commitment to self-love and self-determination. Many people think self-love is ego love, and it is not. Self-love is learning to love yourself at your core, at your inner being and centre, and it is very spiritual. I can still remember the moment I realized that nobody is going to love me the way I want and need to be loved except me. Others can only love me the way they know how to love.

My emotional and physical hardships have been my teachers and they teach me how to own my spirit and my life. Today I take responsibility for my reality and the choices I make. There has been freedom for me in waking up and realizing I am able to overcome obstacles and believe in myself and what I want to create in my life. I am so grateful I have been able to walk through all the layers of healing without using alcohol or substances to deny or change the way I feel. I am aware that

I may have some blind spots not yet uncovered, but I trust myself and have faith that I will know what to do when more might come up. I have learned to not live in constant fear and worry. I am allowing myself to feel peace and joy.

I have also realized that shame has been a major part of my life, and I understand it is just another emotion. I investigated it more deeply as I wrote this book. I realize I felt ashamed of who I was since childhood, and I developed an inner critic. I connected this shame to perfectionism and began to focus on trying to be perfect. However, much of this perfectionism presented itself in my thoughts and feelings and became a constant low level of worry, self-judgement, and inner criticism.

As I continue my growth and self-development, I've become strong enough to make choices that work for me in my life, and I can let go of things and situations that no longer work for me. I have self-compassion on a much deeper level, and I have chosen self-forgiveness in my healing process. I choose to be open to real relationships and to not run or hide from shame. I am learning how to decipher between my shame and another's shame. My resistance to feedback and feeling vulnerable when someone provides me with unsolicited opinions can periodically activate some old layer of shame deep inside me and then I might feel not good enough or smart enough. I need to pause and reassure myself that I am worthy and remind myself it is not about who I am or my essence. This person speaking has

> I realize I walk in two world paradigms, the Indigenous and the Western.

their opinion they want to share, and this is okay, and I am okay. I am in charge and can determine whether I want to use the information or not, but my truth is: *I am worthy*. Much of the inner work I have had to do has been healing and supporting my inner child.

Please feel free to draw or doodle anything that comes up for you. This is your memoir journal.

Journal Space: Where are you on your self-awareness journey or healing journey? Take time to honour yourself and your story and write what it means to you.

The shame has diminished and the feelings of fragility I experience associated with feeling vulnerable become weaker the more I really accept that shame is only a feeling. When I feel vulnerable, I can acknowledge it and comfort myself and talk to someone, and the feeling diminishes. Shame loses its power to live and grow when it is shared with another person for one's healing. Shame lessens its hold on me when I realize I am not abandoned and I am there for myself, I am safe, and I can find ways to comfort and calm myself in positive ways.

Often, when I am about to do something challenging, such as teach a workshop or chair a meeting or speak my truth, I may feel nervous or scared. I know I really want to do what I choose to do, and I know it is just fear and vulnerability affecting me. I have learned not to let this fear and anxiety stop me. Afterward, when I arrive on the other side of an experience or when I have completed the task that I was feeling overwhelmed about, I feel so strong and wonderful. This gives me the internal validation that I am doing the right thing for me, and it brings me feelings of joy, peace, and self-satisfaction. It is a big win for me when I embrace my desire to do something new or let myself be who I truly am; the self-acceptance and self-compassion release the shame and its power over me. This is mostly an inner process that is occurring in myself and when others see me on the outside, it is not what they are seeing. I have been told many times that I present as calm, grounded, and peaceful. I am grateful my insides are now beginning to match my outside. Eventually, I think understanding oneself goes back to the need for us all to really come to love ourselves. The more we do this, the better we can be at loving others in a healthy and respectful way.

I know my decolonization process is my life's journey because of the colonial ways that are so deeply rooted in my psyche. I am working toward releasing the thought processes that continuously perpetuate the duality in thought and behaviour in who I am and how I identify myself. I am Indigenous and will continue the path of self-acceptance and self-determination of who I am and how I experience the world. What I have learned is that my culture is very accepting, and we are left to be who we are meant to be and want to become; it is our own choice and path to follow as we so choose. I know my family and community—as my collective—embraces me as I am, and I am part of a whole. I can understand and empathize when someone is confused or hurting, when someone is feeling oppressed, angry, or frustrated with the political and social context that affects us as Indigenous Peoples here in Canada.

The history of Indigenous Peoples experiencing many abuses that affected them physically, mentally, emotionally, and spiritually in the residential schools is now widespread public knowledge. Healing is occurring simultaneously in families and communities. Because of the historical and intergenerational effects that hurt so many, people are choosing to try several different types of healing to create better lives for themselves right now and for the next generations. The intergenerational trauma is being stopped in some instances. There are leaders, Elders, family members, and organizations that offer information and support for working with those who want to learn what it means to have healthy relationships and respectful interaction with one another. Many are healing from their past victimization that hurt them when they were children and are finding healing for themselves and their families. Healthy sexuality is something that needs to be learned because of all the historical and complex traumas. Brave souls continue to speak outwardly or in safe healing spaces about their experiences with being abused physically, mentally, emotionally, spiritually, and sexually. This is major painful and healing work to do.

I observe others around me who are walking this same path of pursuing their process of decolonization and doing their best to support their loved ones and the collective in their healing. I know that learning to love and heal and be there for my inner child has truly strengthened me and has brought me peace and joy in my life. I have learned to break through the barriers of shame, confusion, and low self-esteem. I live in this colonized world, and I have been able to connect all the pieces and parts of myself together as I walk my life path. My Medicine Wheel is balanced for the most part, and I strive to live in harmony with those who I spend time and work with. When issues arise in relationships and situations, as they do, I can sit in reflection and discern what might be occurring for me and what is the next step I need to make.

I can gently remind myself that I belong, I am perfect and whole, and the external forces of colonialism and structural oppression are real, but I do not have to let them hurt me anymore. I can release myself from those hurtful thoughts and focus on the strength of my culture and its teachings. I remember I am strong, smart, brave, funny, generous, and kind. These are all attributes that come from my cultural teachings. They have not been taken away, and they are in my DNA.

I understand that many of my family and other Indigenous Peoples choose to believe in Jesus and follow organized religious practices, and I accept and respect this reality because this is their choice and path. Moreover, I am open to prayer and support from varying faiths and beliefs people have if I believe and feel they are sharing it with me from a place of love and not trying to convert me. I fully believe in the power of prayer. I have participated in recovery groups that are based in colonial and Christian beliefs and I have been able to find my place and sense of belonging there due to how they are designed. The help they offer is only suggested, and I am free to make my own choices and decisions within these contexts. There is space for me to be who I am and share how I experience and see the world.

However, when I do happen to share about my internalized oppression or racism I've endured, I am aware that I must really take care of myself because I can feel my vulnerability. The stronger I become in my own truth, the less I am affected by uncomfortable feelings. This has all become part of me now, and I feel totally at peace with this. I am pleased to know that I now have full control over how I connect and experience my involvement within my wheel of life.

Several years ago, I was invited into a Sharing Circle of women with a facilitator who was a gifted female Elder. As she shared with us the process of visualization, another woman in the circle who was her helper stood up and sang a women's healing song with her big, beautiful hand drum. As the song began and the drum was played loudly, I closed my eyes and opened my heart. The image of my inner child came out and she was dancing. She was a Fancy Dancer with her beautiful shawl stretched out across her arms, and her regalia and moccasins were so beautiful. I watched her dance freely and she was safe, loved and so beautiful. I sent her love, and I thanked her for trusting me to come out and dance. I know now she is within me, and my adult self loves her deeply. This was a profound healing moment. I love my little girl and she is perfect, whole, and complete. It was a real gift to have this experience, and I feel so happy and peaceful as a result.

> When I have cause, or I am feeling fragile or vulnerable, I can visualize my negative thoughts and emotions and send them away or move them into a space to be dealt with at another time. Each person can create their own visualization of a place of safety in their mind's eye and spirit. Mine is my smudge bowl, so when I light a smudge in my bowl later, I know the negativity will be released and gone. I can stay in the moment I am in and breathe my way forward to happier or more relaxed thoughts and feelings.

This process of coming to understand my cultural reclamation and how it defines me and who I am within it in the context of colonization has been both invigorating and so emotionally draining in some instances. Yet because I have healed so much of my spirit, I feel whole. At times when I am not feeling balanced and strong, I truly must get quiet and talk to myself and love myself enough to gather a sense of what it is I need. Is it to keep moving forward? Is it to rest, pause and take a break? Is it to call someone to talk, or maybe do something nice for someone else? I have many options to choose from on those days or in those moments.

Periodically I feel that being centred or balanced is a constant battle. For example, when I am watching TV or scrolling social media, I see the average commercial and it appears as if Indigenous Peoples are invisible. Most other cultures are represented, but where is my culture? We buy nice big trucks and take vacations too!

Yes, there is poverty and challenges with other social and economic issues, but if you know the history of Canada and the process of how our country was settled, then you can truly see the layers of intergenerational effects we are all overcoming. We each experience this process in our own uniqueness and manner within the family, community, and the collective. So, the decolonization of oneself is personal as well as collective and is continually political.

Journal Space: Do you have any memories that make you feel calm, loved, and good about yourself and your life? Take the time to honour yourself and your story and write what it means to you. What are the ways in which you support your physical, mental, emotional, and spiritual well-being?

My greatest challenge has been to learn to let myself have fun, to feel happy without the worry coming in that something is wrong with me or that something bad is going to happen if I allow myself to be happy. Or there are occasions where I do become affected by past trauma, and I am able to quickly know what I need to do for myself to regain my balance. For example, there were instances as I was writing this memoir that I attended some counselling sessions for my own emotional support. I understand this is connected to living with a history of trauma and with this "internalized oppression anxiety disorder," but I also understand I do not have to listen to these negative or challenging feelings. I know they are there periodically, and I acknowledge their presence, but then I let them flow through me. They are only thoughts and feelings, and I have learned not to attach to them. I take something out of my spiritual bundle to support and love myself in these moments until the negative feelings pass. I understand that if they keep recurring and blocking my happiness, this could be the part of me that needs more love and acceptance. Or it could be there is something I need to investigate deeper to address the lingering emotions and memories that need my attention for more healing.

To this end, I can barely recall some of the past trauma because it has been healed. I also choose not to keep retelling the stories I do remember unless I think I absolutely must. When I make this decision, it is for the possibility of helping someone on their path so that—by hearing some of my story—they might be able to identify, connect, and feel less alone in their pain. I can share some stories from my past without falling apart or re-living the pain. This tells me I am well and have healed from the experiences. If possible, I try to remember to ask permission of the person before I share my personal experiences. Otherwise, I leave it in the past where it belongs.

I started to learn diverse ways to help myself, and to think of myself differently, more positively. I began to internalize different beliefs that helped me change my thinking and behaviour and I have become a more positive and happier person. My spiritual bundle helps me sustain my well-being and further growth.

I have changed. I used to have a negative personality as a pessimist living with many negative thoughts and feelings while enduring many emotionally painful experiences. Eventually I became a person who can process negative feelings and circumstances and move through them and not let them keep me stuck. Now I am finally in a place of joy, self-awareness, acceptance, and love. I have evolved into being an optimist. I know I cannot change my past or history. I cannot change what has happened to me, but I can and do take responsibility for how I continue my healing and keep myself moving forward. My healing has helped me to remember where I come from and to feel proud and strong regarding my culture.

A goal of my personal growth and development has been to make peace with my issues I know came from colonialism and how it affected me in my family of origin story and to honour the strength and character of my parents and family. My sister, other healers, friends, and experiences help me understand much of the Indigenous context and the collective belief systems that I continue to learn more about and process my understanding of them. The language teachers and my mother are helping me to learn more of our language. I feel supported in my continuous journey of decolonization and in my interaction within the two differing paradigms of colonialism and Indigenous ways. I believe there is a need to support one another in how this affects or has affected our relationships and our mental well-being. Compassion, love, and dialogue are key in all circumstances.

> I feel my emotions and observe my thoughts; I can choose how I want to process them. I love and support myself.

My wish is for readers of my memoir journal to know that many of my issues and the circumstances I experienced are directly related to how I internalized systemic oppression and racism associated with being Indigenous and colonized in Canada. Yet, this harsh reality had created within me a personal challenge to overcome. It has been an exceptionally large part of my journey in healing to know and understand, in the words of the late, self-help, self-love guru Louise Hay, "I now choose to begin to see myself as the Universe sees me—perfect, whole, and complete" (Hay, 1999, p. 57).[17] External circumstances had negative effects on me, but they did not break me. Doing my healing through inner work and embracing my cultural reclamation has helped me learn to love myself and be self-determined.

I finally realized this is my truth and what I bring into the circle. This is my strength and my passion that I share. I am confident and safe in my own spirit and personality. I accept that I have been colonized and will continue to forge forward while making sense of living in two worlds and understanding the Indigenous culture I belong to. I am grateful for my life and all the different blessings I have today and the challenges I have had to overcome. I know that as long as I stay close to my Creator and use what is in my spiritual bundle, I am okay, and I will be okay. I look forward to continuing my Medicine Wheel journey—this journey of living and being true to who I am.

This brings me to the end of my memoir journal. I say miigwech for coming with me through the literature that I gathered and applied to my own circumstance as I completed my academic journey. My hope is that we all continue to know we are so worthy. External circumstances can play havoc in our lives, but we are strong, resilient, and free to overcome them.

Notes

1   Currie, C., Wild, C., Schopflocher, D., & Laing, L. (2015). Racial discrimination, post-traumatic stress and prescription drug problems among Aboriginal Canadians. *Canadian Journal of Public Health*, 106 (6): e382-e387.
2   Ray, S. (1981). *The only diet there is.* Celestial Arts.
3   Bopp, J., Bopp, M., Brown, L., & Lane, P. (2003). *The sacred tree* (3rd ed.). Four Worlds Development Press.
4   Lavallee, B., & Clearsky, L. (2006). From woundedness to resilience: A critical review from an Aboriginal perspective. *Journal of Aboriginal Health*, September 4-6.
5   Heilbron, C. L., & Guttman, M. A. (2000). The traditional healing methods with First Nations women in group counselling. *Canadian Journal of Counselling*, 34(1), 3-13.
6   Oulanova, O., & Moodley, R. (2010). Navigating two worlds: Experiences of counsellors who integrate Aboriginal traditional healing practices. *Canadian Journal of Counselling and Psychotherapy*, 44 (4), 346-362.
7   Dyck, N., & Sadik, T. (2011). Indigenous political organization and activism in Canada. *The Canadian Encyclopedia*. Retrieved May 12, 2023, from https://www.thecanadianencyclopedia.ca/en/article/aboriginal-people-political-organization-and-activism
8   Elias, B., Mignone, J., Hall, M., Hong, S.P., Hart, L., & Sareen, J. (2012). Trauma and suicide behaviour histories among a Canadian Indigenous population: An empirical exploration of the potential role of Canada's residential school system. *Social Science & Medicine*, 74: 1560-1569.
9   Bombay, A., Matheson, K., & Anisman, H. (2014). The intergenerational effects of Indian residential schools: Implications for the concept of historical trauma. *Transcultural Psychiatry*, 51(3), 320-338.
10 Kirmayer, L.J., Brass, G.M., & Tait, C.L. (2000). The mental health of Aboriginal peoples: Transformation of identity and community. *Canadian Journal of Psychiatry*, 45, September, 607-616.
11 Hallowell, A.I. (1992). *The Ojibwa of Berens River, Manitoba: Ethnography in history.* Harcourt Brace Jovanovich College Publishers.
12 Rowe, S., Baldry, E., & Earles, W. (2015). Decolonizing social work research: Learning from critical Indigenous approaches. *Australian Social Work*, 68 (3). 296-308.

13 Linklater, R. (2014). *Decolonizing trauma work: Indigenous stories and strategies.* Fernwood Publishing.

14 Ermine, W. (2007). The ethical space of engagement. *Indigenous Law Journal,* 6 (1). 193-203.

15 Overmars, D. (2010). Diagnosis as a naming ceremony: Caution warranted in use of the DSM-IV with Canadian Aboriginal Peoples. *First Peoples Child & Family Review,* 5(1), 78-85. Retrieved from https://fpcfr.com/index.php/FPCFR/article/view/176

16 White Bison (2002). *The red road to wellbriety in the Native American way.* White Bison Inc.

17 Hay, L (1999). *You can heal your life.* Hay House Inc.

Bibliography

Absolon, K. (2010). Indigenous wholistic theory: A knowledge set for practice. *First Peoples Child & Family Review,* 5, (2), 74-87.

Absolon, K.E. (2016). Wholistic and ethical: Social inclusion with Indigenous peoples. *Social Inclusion,* 4, 1, 44-56.

Alfred, G.T. (2009). Colonialism and state dependency. *Journal of Aboriginal Health,* 5 (2). 42-60.

Baines, D. (2007). *Doing anti-oppressive practice: Building transformative politicized social work.* Fernwood Publishing.

Boksa, P., Joober, R., & Kirmayer, L.J. (2015). Mental wellness in Canada's Aboriginal communities: Striving toward reconciliation. *Journal of Psychiatry and Neuroscience,* 40(6), 363-365.

Bourassa, C., McKay-McNabb, K., & Hampton, M. (2004). Racism, sexism, and colonialism: The Impact of the health of Aboriginal women in Canada. *Canadian Women Studies,* 24 (1), 23-29.

Bransford, C.L. (2011). Integrating critical consciousness into direct social work practice: A pedagogical view. *Social Work Education,* 30:8, 932-947.

Brown, B. (2012). *Daring greatly: How the courage to be vulnerable transforms the way we live, love, parent and lead.* Penguin Group (USA) Inc.

Carriere, J., & Richardson, C. (2013). Relationship is everything: Holistic approaches to Aboriginal child and youth mental health. *First Peoples Child & Family Review,* 7(2). 8-26. https://doi.org/10.7202/1068837ar

Clifford, D. (2016). Oppression and professional ethics. *Ethics and Social Welfare,* 10:1, 4-18, DOI: 10.1080/17496535.2015.1072225

Corey, G., Schneider Cory, M., Callanan, P., & Russell, J. (2015). *Group techniques 4th edition.* Cengage Learning.

Dee Watts-Jones, T. (2010). Location of self: Opening the door to dialogue on intersectionality in the therapy process. *Family Process,* 49 (3),405-420.

Diangelo, Robin. (2018). *White fragility: Why it's so hard for white people to talk about racism.* Beacon Press.

Fontaine, T. (2010). *Broken circle: The dark legacy of indian residential schools.* Heritage House Publishing Company Ltd.

Gone, J. P. (2013). Redressing First Nations historical trauma: Theorizing mechanisms for Indigenous culture as mental health treatment. *Transcultural Psychiatry*, 50(5), 683-706.

Graham, H., & Leeseberg Stamler, L. (2010). Contemporary perceptions of health from an Indigenous (Plains Cree) perspective. *Journal of Aboriginal Health*, 6 (1), 6-17.

Hart, M.A. (1996). Sharing circles: Utilizing traditional practise methods for teaching, helping and supporting. In O'Meara, S. West, D.A. (Eds.). *From our eyes: Learning from Indigenous peoples*, pp. 59-72. Garamond Press.

Hart, M.A. (2002). *Seeking mino-pitmatisiwin: An aboriginal approach to helping*. Fernwood Publishing. Chapter 2, 23-37.

Heart, M.Y., & Debruyn, L.M. (1998). The American Indian holocaust: Healing historical unresolved grief. *American Indian and Alaska Native Mental Health Research: Journal of the National Center*, 8 (2), 56-78.

Kading, M.L., Hautala, D.S., Palombi, LC., Aronson, B.D., Smith, R.C., & Walls, M.L. (2015). Flourishing: American Indian Positive Mental Health. *Society and Mental Health, American Sociological Association*, 5(3), 203-217.

Kirmayer, L.J. (2012). Cultural competence and evidence-based practice in mental health: Epistemic communities and the politics of pluralism. *Social Science & Medicine*, 75: 249-256.

Kirmayer, L.J., Brass, G.M., & Tait, C.L. (2000). The mental health of Aboriginal peoples: Transformation of identity and community. *Canadian Journal of Psychiatry*, 45, September, 607-616.

Kirmayer, L.J., Rousseau, C., & Guzder, J. (2014). Introduction: The place of culture in mental health services. In Kirmayer, L., Guzder, J., Rousseau, C. (Eds.), *Cultural consultation: Encountering the other in mental health care*, 1-20, International and Cultural Psychology, Springer.

Knight, C. (2006). Groups for individuals with traumatic histories: Practice considerations for social workers. *National Association of Social Workers*, 51 (1): 20-30).

Knight, C. (2015). Trauma-informed social work practice: Practice considerations and challenges. *Journal of Clinical Social Work Practice*, 43 (1):25-37.

Liu, J.H., Lawson-Te Aho, K., & Rata, A. (2014). Constructing identity spaces for First Nations people: Towards an Indigenous psychology of self-determination and cultural healing. *Psychology and Developmental Societies*, 26(2) 143-153.

MCSW. (2021). *Social work code of ethics and guidelines for ethical practice*.

Manitoba College of Social Workers (MCSW). Reproduced with permission from Canadian Association of Social Workers (2005), Social Work Code of Ethics.

Mate, G. (2009). *In the realm of hungry ghosts: Close encounters with addiction.* North Atlantic Books.

McCabe, G. (2008). Mind, body, emotions and spirit: Reaching to the ancestors for healing. *Counselling Psychology Quarterly,* 21, (2), 143-152.

Morrisseau, C. (2008). *Into the daylight: A wholistic approach to healing.* University Toronto Press Incorporated.

Nabigon, H. (2007). *The hollow tree: Fighting addiction with traditional native healing.* McGill-Queen's University Press.

Neeganagwedgin, D.E. (2014). They can't take our ancestors out of us: A brief historical account of Canada's residential school system, incarceration, institutionalized policies and legislations against Indigenous peoples. *Canadian Issues,* Spring: 31-36.

Newton, K. (2010). A two-fold unveiling: Unmasking classism in group work. *The Journal for Specialists in Group Work,* 35:3, 212-219.

Ratts, M.J., & Santos, K.N.T. (2010). The dimensions of social justice model: Transforming traditional group work into a socially just framework. *The Journal for Specialists in Group Work,* 35:2, 160-168.

Reeves, A., & Stewart, S.L. (2015). Exploring the integration of Indigenous healing and western psychotherapy for sexual trauma survivors who use mental health services at Anishnawbe Health Toronto. *Canadian Journal of Counselling and Psychotherapy,* 49(1), 57-78.

Robbins, J. A., & Dewar, J. (2011). Traditional Indigenous approaches to healing and the modern welfare of traditional knowledge, spirituality and lands: A critical reflection on practices and policies take from the Canadian Indigenous example. *The International Indigenous Policy Journal,* 2 (4).

Rothchild, B. (2010). *8 keys to safe trauma recovery: Take-charge strategies to empower your healing.* W. W. Norton & Company, Inc.

Roy, V., & Pullen-Sansfaçon, A. (2016). Promoting individual and social changes: A hybrid model of social work with groups. *Social Work with Groups,* 39 (1), 4-20.

Singh, A.A., Merchant, N., Skudrzyk, B., & Ingene, D. (2012). Association for specialists in group work: Multicultural and social justice competence principles for group workers. *The Journal for Specialists in Group Work,* 37(4), 312-325.

Singh, A.A., & Salazar, C.F. (2010). Six considerations for social justice group work. *The Journal for Specialists in Group Work*, 35 (3), 308-319.

Stewart, S. (2009). Family counselling as decolonization: Exploring an Indigenous social-constructivist approach in clinical practice. *First Peoples Child & Family Review*, 4 (1), 62-70.

Tipping, C. (2010). *Radical forgiveness: A revolutionary five-stage process to heal relationships, let go of anger and blame, and find peace in any situation*. Sounds True.

Toseland, R., & Rivas, R. (2012). *An introduction to group work practice* (7th Ed). Allyn and Bacon.

Verniest, L. (2006). Allying with the medicine wheel: Social work practice with Aboriginal peoples. *Journal of Critical Social Work*, 7 (1), 1-12.

Waldram, J.B. (2013). Transformative and restorative processes: Revisiting the question of efficacy of Indigenous healing. *Medical Anthropology*, 32(3), 191-207.

Waldram, J. B., Herring, A. D., & Young, T. K. (2006). *Aboriginal health in Canada: Historical, cultural, and epidemiological perspectives.* (2nd Ed). University of Toronto Press.

Weiss, D. Ph.D. (2016). *Intimacy anorexia: Healing the hidden addiction in your marriage*. Discovery Press.

Wendt, D. C., Gone, J. P., & Kirmayer, L. J. (2012). Rethinking cultural competence: Insights from Indigenous community treatment settings. *Transcultural Psychiatry*, 49(2), 206-222.

Younging, G. (2018). *Elements of indigenous style: A guide for writing by and about indigenous peoples*. Brush Education.

Appendix – Questions for Reflecting on Self-Care Within One's Medicine Wheel

Physical / Material Aspects:

In what condition is my physical health?

What are my physical needs right now?

What does my body language tell me? Do I like myself?

What are my priorities to improve my physical well-being?

What positive activities can I enjoy to enhance my physical well-being in the areas of nutrition, sleep, exercise, appearance, posture, rest & relaxation, clothing, home tidiness, or financial situation?

What harmful things (e.g., various dependencies) must I avoid to achieve health?

What do I see about my future on the physical and on the material planes?

What are my goals? How do I see myself in two years from now?

Mental / Intellectual / Cognitive Aspects

What is my self-talk?

What are my general intellectual activities?

What are the mental stimulations (e.g., creative activities, reading, studying,) in my life?

What are my creative abilities and how do I foster them?

Am I satisfied with my level of education as well as intellectual and cognitive development?

Am I satisfied with the kind of work I am doing?

Do I take time to reflect and analyze what is happening in my life?

What are my problem-solving skills and how can I improve them?

Is time management a problem in life?

Emotional / Social / Relational Aspects:

In what condition is my emotional health?

What are my emotional needs at this time?

Do I have positive self-esteem and a strong sense of self-worth?

Am I able to express my feelings and do I have someone to confide in?

Do I trust people?

Do I feel the need to control other people or situations?

Am I maintaining healthy relationships (e.g., with my life partner, family, relatives, friends, co-workers, neighbours)?

Am I comfortable with my own sexuality?

Am I in an intimate relationship that is healthy or unhealthy?

Am I open to being in an intimate relationship? Why or why not?

What are my coping strategies?

What positive things can I do to enhance my emotional and social well-being?

Am I taking time to nurture the relationships in my life?

Do I have unresolved issues from the past?

What do I feel about the future?

Spiritual / Ethical / Cultural Aspects:

Do I have meaning and purpose in my life?

Do I live up to my principles, beliefs, and values?

Do I have any spiritual / religious beliefs and practices? What are they?

Do I take time out for prayer, fasting, silence, meditation, or enjoyment of nature?

Do I have a grateful attitude about life?

Do I fear death and dying, and, if so, for what reason(s)?

Am I honest, loving, caring, sharing, respectful, trustworthy, humble, and helpful?

In what ways am I respectful of nature?

Do I feel a sense of connectedness and pride for the values of my culture?

What positive activities can I do to nurture my spiritual life?

Adapted from the work of Loiselle, Margot, PhD SW, and McKenzie, Lauretta, MSW. Workshop conducted on May 27, 2006, at Renison University College, Waterloo, Ontario.

About the Author

Annette Alix Roussin holds a Master of Social Work from the University of Manitoba and has spent her career working with others in both the health and education sectors with a focus on mental health and well-being. Annette is a licensed Heal Your Life Teacher and has been certified with the Coach U Life Coach Core Essentials Program.

Annette is of Ojibway descent and is a registered citizen of Miimiiwiziibiing (Berens River First Nation) Treaty No. 5 in Manitoba. Annette brings to her relationships her understanding of the core values from her Indigenous culture of love, respect, courage, honesty, wisdom, humility, and truth.

Annette believes each person has their own journey to walk to find self-love, peace, and balance in their lives, and it is by doing this inner work and self-development that one can find what they need to break through to new possibilities and adventures. Each one of us must find the way on this life journey and Annette loves to be a witness, a safe space, a mentor, and supporter for those who are seeking their own truth and balance in their life.

Visit www.foreverevolving.ca to learn more about Annette.

This book was amazing to me. It catches your attention from the first page and captures your thinking in ways you don't normally think. I can well imagine that if you are seeking a memoir that supports journaling and self-healing, this book would be so valuable and re-affirming. As a result, once I started, I didn't stop. And then I came back to it and did it again.

—*Dr. Catherine Cook*
Vice-President (Indigenous), University of Manitoba

This is an act of courage. Courage to own your story, and to situate your story within the framework of time and history. Get yourself prepared. Offer tobacco and find a safe place. This work is not easy. It will take many steps and you'll need to visit and revisit parts of yourself. It is not quickly done, but it's worth it. It is a gift you make to yourself and to your circle of caring. This is an act of generosity by Annette to give you milestones on her journey to guide you. Remember to make room for this work to grow into the fabric of your life. Become what the ancestors dreamed for you. Aho.

—*Louis Sorin*
Red Buffalo Man

I used to have what I call the typical or common view of Indigenous Peoples and how they see life. In my mind, I could not understand why they did not simply move on; after all, residential schools were "over years ago." I also used to believe it was wrong for my generation to continue to pay for the sins of my forefathers.

Thanks to Annette, I now have a new pair of glasses through which I see these things. I understand historical and intergenerational trauma are not just catch phrases but are very real and run deep and strong in Indigenous cultures. One cannot do things differently if they do not know there is a different way to do things.

—*Judi McFarland*
Administrative Assistant, St. Boniface Hospital

www.ingramcontent.com/pod-product-compliance
Lightning Source LLC
Chambersburg PA
CBHW020158090426
42734CB00008B/868